"STOP COMPLAINING ABOUT YOUR JOB? GET OUT THERE & HUSTLE!"

CHAPTER 1: THE WAKE-UP CALL

Realizing your worth and potential.

Signs You are Stuck: Identifying if you are in a dead-end job.

The First Steps: The moment of clarity and deciding to make a change.

CHAPTER 2: DITCHING THE DUMMY BOSS

Recognizing Toxic Leadership: How to spot a dummy boss.

The Great Escape: Planning your escape plan.

Breaking Up Gracefully: Quitting without burning bridges.

CHAPTER 3: FIND YOUR PASSION, NOT ANOTHER JOB

Self-Discovery: Tools and exercises to find what you truly love.

The Passion Economy: Understanding how to monetize your interests.

Aligning Values and Work: Making sure your new path resonates with your personal values.

CHAPTER 4: THE FREELANCER'S PLAYBOOK

Freelancing Basics: How to start freelancing in your field

.

Building a Client Base: Networking and finding your first clients.

Managing Freelance Life: Tips for staying productive and organized.

CHAPTER 5: ENTREPRENEURIAL MINDSET

Thinking Like a Boss: Shifting from employee to entrepreneur mindset.

Risk and Reward: Understanding and managing the risks of entrepreneurship.

Innovation and Creativity: Leveraging your unique ideas.

CHAPTER 6: SIDE HUSTLES TO MAIN HUSTLES

Starting Small: How to begin with a side hustle.

Scaling Up: Transitioning from side hustle to full-time business.

Case Studies: Success stories of people who turned hobbies into careers.

CHAPTER 7: BUILDING YOUR BRAND

Personal Branding: Crafting your image and message.

Social media: Utilizing social platforms to grow your brand.

Content is King: Creating valuable content that attracts an audience.

CHAPTER 8: FINANCIAL FREEDOM

Budgeting for Independence: Managing your finances when you are your own boss.

Investment Strategies: Growing your wealth beyond a regular paycheck.

Emergency Funds and Savings: Preparing for financial uncertainties.

CHAPTER 9: THE NETWORK EFFECT

Building Connections: Effective networking strategies.

Mentorship and Guidance: Finding and leveraging mentors.

Collaborations and Partnerships: Working with others for mutual benefit.

CHAPTER 10: OVERCOMING SETBACKS

Handling Failure: Learning from mistakes and moving forward.

Stress Management: Techniques to stay sane during the entrepreneurial journey.

Persistence Pays Off: Stories of perseverance and success after failure.

CHAPTER 11: THE DIGITAL NOMAD LIFE

Remote Work Essentials: Tools and tips for working from anywhere.

Travel and Work: Balancing work with the digital nomad lifestyle.

Cultural Adaptability: Embracing and thriving in different cultures.

CHAPTER 12: PAYING IT FORWARD

Teaching and Mentoring: Helping others start their own journeys.Giving Back: Philanthropy and social responsibility.

Legacy Building: Creating something that outlasts you.

Conclusion: Take the Leap

Motivational words to inspire immediate action.

Additional tools and books for continued growth.

CHAPTER 1: THE WAKE-UP CALL

Realizing your worth and potential.

One of our most basic needs is to feel accepted and liked. Even more critical is that we like and accept ourselves. Self-acceptance leads to feelings of greater happiness and well-being. It allows us to enjoy a balanced, rewarding, and gratifying life. Self-acceptance is a great accomplishment for many people. They undervalue themselves, deprive themselves of decent rewards, and remove other pathways to emotional well-being. Then, over time, they accept this blighted emotional state as the norm, feel life is a series of broken dreams drifting endlessly to the unexpected end. They judge their self-worth by what they own or by the success that others define for them.

This pattern leads to insecurity, and it is difficult to reach self-acceptance. Desiring success and working hard for what you want is important; however, accepting yourself rather than the superficial attachments and trappings of life tells others how to value you as well. Rethinking your self-worth involves changing your self-evaluations to a status that feels more rewarding. Your level of self-worth can significantly change your life.

In a society that places so much value on celebrity and personal "brand," it can be exceedingly difficult for the average person to feel important or valued. So much importance is attached to wealth and beauty, and people are very often judged by these two factors. While it is true that a person who is physically appealing and who has a lot of money may be able to move through life more smoothly than those who do not have these attributes, it is also true that neither money nor beauty make a person better than another person.

That is not something that many people really believe, however. In fact, most of us harbor some undervalued beliefs about ourselves that can lead to feelings of low self-worth. A poor self-image is at the core of many of the problems that people encounter, from working at a job that makes them unhappy or staying in a troubled marriage, to not even trying to make changes in their lives that would benefit them and make them happier. Believing in your worth and potential is a critical first step to living a successful life.

Recognizing your unique skills and talents

Chatting with friends, family members, complete strangers, self-awareness exercises are just a part of activities were discovering true passions and developing skills will help you get to know yourself better. Bring your uniqueness to the surface, believe in yourself because that is what makes you extraordinary.

Your uniqueness is a combination of gifts from which you stand out and are better at than other people. The easiest way to identify your abilities and talents is to make a list of skills you possess. Start writing down the things you have passion about and the things that you do well in the particular area.

You could have fun making new recipes or playing games— abilities continue to emerge in everyone. People will consider that the things you do better than other people are not that important. Changing your perspective will change the way you think about your special talent. Know yourself well enough to recognize and use your unique skills that could bring you success.

Everyone has unique skills and talents, known as occupational ability, which can be realized through an occupation or activity in which they have a special interest. Realizing your worth and potential also requires reflecting on your life. Showing who you truly are and standing for your uniqueness can be scary because of high social expectations, beliefs, and stereotypes we put on ourselves. Such fears bring us into a powerless state in which we feel restricted, lost, and unable to act. Leaving the comfort zone is not easy, but it is crucial to stay true to ourselves. To start respecting this uniqueness, it is important to discover what kind of skills and talents you have.

Identifying your personal strengths and qualities

To identify or choose our main qualities, we can ask ourselves these questions: Among the new skills related to the employment sector, which ones are the most popular and the most sought after? Are there any technical skills or work experience, useful to be part of an expert team, valued by both national and international networks of experts? Our resilience, despite what circumstances and adversaries bring into our lives, reflects our ability to overcome shocks and accept to adapt to shocks. It allows us to continue to have life projects and plans despite difficulties and to achieve our goals and ambitions. Resilience does not mean suspending the feeling of sadness, anger, and other emotions when they arise. We had the time that we all needed to accept and express our feelings.

We all have personal strengths and qualities that make us unique. When we must complete a challenging task, one of these strengths may help us to achieve it. But sometimes we pretend that we do not have any and do not realize that the very fact of always being able to complete a list of tasks and having to display an unbelievable amount of resilient endurance in doing so is a great strength. Often, it helps to ask a person we trust to help us identify our personal strengths and qualities. If we take the time and a little thought or research, we can find many things we are good at, or that we have acquired about which we can be proud. These can be examples of resilience, personality strengths, or other kinds of skills and knowledge.

Acknowledging your past achievements and successes

For example, if you doubt whether there is anything that you have done that you are proud of, then an effective way to remind yourself is to go back to the time when you were born and document at least two things for every year of your life. If you cannot remember much about your life, talk to other people. A problem that you might run into is that some of the things that you were proud of might have been negative.

Now, you might be thinking, "Can I include that?" No, you should not include that. However, what fields or career paths might have framed those activities consider to be inspired ideas or determined hard-worker or ambitious person activities. If you were to re-frame them based on how those achievements have achieved past or current goals, then they can feed into the positive reinforcement you are trying to build to become confident or a different kind of person, and to challenge negative self-defeating attitudes.

When you reflect on your life, you realize that the journey has been long, and there are numerous achievements that you might not be proud of at all. However, you ought to remember that you have also done some things that you are proud of and if you have done one thing, you can do more things of which you are proud. You ought to acknowledge the achievements that you are proud of on purpose in connection to the fact that believing in your potential and in the fact that you are deserving is a choice, which is something the next chapter explores. It is something you do regardless of your drawbacks and faults. Therefore, purposeful reflection feeds into the power you need to intentionally believe in yourself. Without it, your manner of shifting your mindset change might come across as saying empty positive mantras, which you might see as a waste of time.

Signs You are Stuck: Identifying if you are in a dead-end job.

Identifying whether you are in a dead-end job is crucial for maintaining your professional satisfaction and growth. I begin by examining the potential for career advancement within my current role and organization. If there are limited opportunities for progression or if promotions seem out of reach, it is a significant indicator that I might be in a dead-end job. Dead-end roles often lack clear paths for advancement, leaving employees feeling stagnant and unfulfilled.

Another key aspect I consider is the level of engagement and enthusiasm I feel towards my work. If I find myself consistently disinterested or unmotivated by my tasks, it could suggest that I am stuck in a dead-end job. Dead-end positions tend to involve repetitive, mundane tasks that offer little challenge or stimulation, leading to a decline in job satisfaction and overall morale.

I also pay close attention to the learning and development opportunities available to me within the company. Dead-end jobs typically lack training programs or initiatives aimed at honing employees' skills and expanding their knowledge base. Without opportunities for growth and learning, employees can quickly become stagnant in their roles, hindering their long-term career prospects.

Furthermore, I assess the overall stability and trajectory of the organization I work for. If the company is struggling financially or experiencing frequent turnover, it could indicate that I am in a dead-end job. Dead-end positions often lack job security and may leave employees vulnerable to layoffs or downsizing during times of uncertainty.

Additionally, I consider the level of compensation and benefits offered in my current role. While dead-end jobs may provide a steady source of income in the short term, they often come with lower wages and limited benefits compared to roles with more opportunities for advancement. This can have long-term implications for financial stability and career growth.

Moreover, I evaluate the work-life balance provided by my job. Dead-end positions may require long hours or involve stress without offering adequate compensation or support. If my job negatively impacts my personal life or mental well-being without offering any potential for advancement, it could be a sign that I am in a dead-end situation.

Pros and cons exist within the realm of dead-end jobs, though they often weigh heavily on one side of the scale. On the positive side, dead-end jobs can provide a steady source of income and stability in the short term.

They may also offer a predictable routine, which can be comforting for some individuals. Additionally, dead-end jobs can serve as a temporary steppingstone while exploring other career options or pursuing further education. However, the cons of working in a dead-end job can outweigh these benefits.

One major drawback is the lack of fulfillment and satisfaction that comes from feeling stuck in a role with no room for growth or advancement. Dead-end jobs can also lead to feelings of stagnation and boredom, which can negatively impact overall job satisfaction and mental well-being. Furthermore, there is the risk of becoming trapped in a cycle of low-paying, unfulfilling work, which can hinder long-term career prospects and financial stability. Additionally, dead-end jobs may not offer competitive benefits or job security, leaving employees vulnerable to unexpected layoffs or downsizing.

In conclusion, identifying whether you are in a dead-end job requires careful consideration of several factors, including career advancement opportunities, job satisfaction, learning and development initiatives, organizational stability, compensation and benefits, and work-life balance. By assessing these aspects critically, you can determine whether your current role aligns with your long-term career goals and aspirations, allowing you to make informed decisions about your professional future.

The First Steps: The moment of clarity and deciding to make a change.

The moment of clarity, that instant when everything suddenly becomes clear, can be a powerful catalyst for change in one's life. For me, it was a convergence of several factors that culminated in a profound realization that I needed to make a change. It might have been a culmination of dissatisfaction with my current circumstances, a desire for something more fulfilling, or simply an acknowledgment of my own potential and the realization that I was not living up to it.

In that moment of clarity, I found myself reflecting deeply on my goals, values, and aspirations. I asked myself to probe questions about what truly mattered to me and whether my current path was aligning with those values. It was a moment of introspection that allowed me to see beyond the immediate challenges and frustrations of my situation and envision a future that resonated more deeply with who I wanted to be.

Deciding to make a change was not easy. It required courage, self-awareness, and a willingness to step outside of my comfort zone. But in that moment of clarity, I realized that staying stagnant was no longer an option. I owed it to myself to pursue a path that was more authentic and fulfilling, even if it meant facing uncertainty and taking risks along the way.

Once I made the decision to change, there was a profound sense of liberation and empowerment that washed over me. It was as if a weight had been lifted off my shoulders, and I felt a newfound sense of purpose and determination coursing through my veins. I was no longer beholden to the constraints of my past decisions or the expectations of others. I was free to carve out my own path and pursue my dreams with unwavering resolve.

Of course, making a change also meant confronting fear and doubt head-on. There were moments of hesitation and second-guessing, as well as setbacks and challenges along the way. But in those moments, I drew strength from the clarity of my vision and the unwavering conviction that I was on the right path. I refused to let fear hold me back or allow doubt to undermine my progress. I forged ahead with determination and resilience, knowing that the journey would be fraught with obstacles but worth it in the end.

Looking back, I can say with certainty that the moment of clarity and the decision to make a change were pivotal turning points in my life. They set me on a trajectory of growth, self-discovery, and fulfillment that continues to unfold to this day. And while the road ahead may still be uncertain at times, I take comfort in knowing that I have the clarity of purpose and the courage to face whatever challenges come my way.

CHAPTER 2: DITCHING THE DUMMY BOSS

Recognizing Toxic Leadership: How to spot a dummy boss

Recognizing toxic leadership is essential for maintaining a healthy work environment and preserving one's well-being. I have learned to identify the signs of toxic leadership through personal experience and observation. One of the most telling indicators is a lack of transparency and communication from upper management. When leaders withhold information, make decisions behind closed doors, or fail to communicate openly with their team, it creates a culture of mistrust and uncertainty.

Another red flag is an authoritarian leadership style characterized by micromanagement and a refusal to delegate tasks. Toxic bosses often exert control over every aspect of their team's work, leaving employees feeling disempowered and undervalued. Additionally, they may exhibit manipulative or bullying behavior, using intimidation tactics to assert their authority and silence dissent.

To spot a "dummy boss," as I call them, I look for signs of incompetence or a lack of qualifications for their role. This might manifest as a failure to understand the intricacies of the job, an inability to make informed decisions, or a general disregard for best practices and industry standards. Dummy bosses may rely on superficial measures of success, such as arbitrary metrics or flashy presentations, rather than focusing on meaningful outcomes and long-term strategy.

Moreover, I pay attention to how leaders manage feedback and criticism. Toxic bosses often react defensively or dismissively when confronted with constructive feedback, refusing to acknowledge their mistakes or take responsibility for their actions. They may also engage in scapegoating, blaming others for their own shortcomings or failures, rather than holding themselves accountable.

Furthermore, I assess the impact of leadership behavior on the overall culture of the organization. Toxic leaders create a toxic work environment characterized by fear, stress, and low morale. Employees may feel demotivated, disengaged, or even physically and mentally unwell because of their interactions with toxic bosses. High turnover rates and a lack of loyalty among staff are common consequences of toxic leadership.

To address toxic leadership, it is important to speak up and advocate for change. This might involve providing feedback to upper management, seeking support from HR or other resources within the organization, or even considering leaving the toxic environment altogether. It is also crucial to prioritize self-care and establish boundaries to protect one's well-being in the face of toxic leadership.

Ultimately, recognizing toxic leadership requires a combination of awareness, observation, and courage to act. By identifying the signs of toxicity and advocating for positive change, individuals can help create a healthier, more productive work environment for themselves and their colleagues.

The Great Escape: Planning your escape plan.

Planning your escape plan from a dead-end job requires careful consideration and strategic thinking. The first step is to assess your current situation and identify the specific reasons why you feel stuck in your role. This might involve reflecting on your career goals, aspirations, and values, as well as evaluating the opportunities for growth and advancement within your organization. By gaining clarity on what you want to achieve and why your current job is not fulfilling those objectives, you can begin to formulate a plan for moving forward.

Once you have identified the reasons for wanting to leave your dead-end job, the next step is to set clear goals and objectives for your escape plan. This might include establishing a timeline for when you want to leave your current job, outlining the steps you need to take to transition to a new role or career path, and identifying any resources or support networks that can help you along the way. Setting concrete goals and objectives will provide you with a roadmap to follow as you navigate the process of leaving your dead-end job.

One important aspect of planning your escape plan is to build a strong professional network that can support you in your job search and career transition. This might involve reaching out to former colleagues, mentors, industry contacts, and other professionals who can provide advice, referrals, and opportunities for networking and job leads. Building and nurturing your professional network will increase your chances of finding new job opportunities and making a successful transition to a more fulfilling career.

Additionally, it is important to update your resume, LinkedIn profile, and other professional materials to reflect your skills, experience, and career objectives. Tailoring your resume and online presence to highlight your strengths and accomplishments will make you more attractive to potential employers and help you stand out in a competitive job market. Consider seeking feedback from trusted colleagues, mentors, or career advisors to ensure that your materials effectively display your qualifications and expertise.

As you plan your escape plan, it is also important to consider your financial situation and make any necessary preparations to ensure a smooth transition. This might involve saving money to cover living expenses during a period of unemployment, researching potential job opportunities and salary ranges in your desired field, and exploring options for additional education or training to enhance your skills and qualifications. By proactively addressing financial considerations, you can minimize the stress and uncertainty of leaving your dead-end job and increase your chances of success in your career transition.

Another important aspect of planning your escape plan is to consider the emotional impact of leaving your current job and transitioning to a new role or career path. It is normal to experience feelings of fear, doubt, and uncertainty when making a major life change, but it is important to recognize that these feelings are a natural part of the process. Take time to acknowledge and process your emotions, and seek support from friends, family, or a therapist if needed. Remember that leaving your dead-end job is a positive step towards creating a more fulfilling and satisfying career, and that you deserve to pursue your passions and aspirations.

In addition to addressing the practical and emotional aspects of planning your escape plan, it is also important to stay focused and motivated throughout the process. Set small, achievable goals for yourself, celebrate your successes along the way, and stay committed to your long-term vision for your career. Remember that leaving your dead-end job is a process, and that it may take time and effort to achieve your goals. Stay persistent, stay positive, and stay true to yourself as you navigate the challenges and opportunities of your career transition.

Finally, as you plan your escape plan from your dead-end job, it is important to remain flexible and adaptable in your approach. Unexpected challenges and opportunities may arise along the way, and it is important to be open to new possibilities and willing to adjust your plans as needed. By staying flexible and maintaining a cheerful outlook, you can navigate the difficulties of your career transition with confidence and resilience and achieve success in your efforts to leave your dead-end job and pursue a more fulfilling and rewarding career path.

Breaking Up Gracefully: Quitting without burning bridges

Quitting a job without burning bridges requires careful planning, professionalism, and tact. As I contemplate leaving my current position, I recognize the importance of maintaining positive relationships with my colleagues and employer, even as I transition to a new role or career path. One of the key principles guiding my approach is to give ample notice of my resignation. By providing my employer with sufficient time to find a replacement and transition my responsibilities, I demonstrate respect for their needs and minimize the disruption caused by my departure.

In addition to giving notice, I strive to communicate my decision to leave in a clear, honest, and professional manner. I scheduled a meeting with my supervisor to discuss my resignation and express my gratitude for the opportunities I have had while working at the company. I avoid placing blame or criticizing the organization, focusing instead on my own career goals and aspirations. By framing my decision as a positive step towards personal and professional growth, I help ensure that my departure is viewed in a constructive light.

During the transition period, I tried to tie up loose ends and complete any outstanding projects or tasks to the best of my ability. I offer to assist with training my replacement and provide detailed documentation to help ensure a smooth handover of responsibilities. By demonstrating my commitment to leaving my role in good standing and setting up my successor for success, I help mitigate any negative impact my departure may have on the organization.

Throughout the resignation process, I remain professional and courteous in my interactions with colleagues and supervisors. I avoid gossiping or spreading negativity about the company or my coworkers, and I refrain from making disparaging remarks on social media or other public forums. Instead, I focus on maintaining positive relationships and leaving an impression of professionalism and integrity.

After leaving my job, I stay in touch with former colleagues and supervisors, keeping the lines of communication open for potential networking opportunities or future collaborations. I express my gratitude for the support and mentorship I received during my time at the company, and I offer my assistance if needed in the future. By nurturing these relationships, I leave the door open for potential opportunities down the road and ensure that I remain in good standing with my former employer and coworkers.

In some cases, I may choose to provide constructive feedback to my employer as part of the resignation process. This feedback is offered in a spirit of goodwill and with the intention of helping the organization improve and grow. I focus on providing specific, actionable suggestions for areas of improvement, rather than dwelling on past grievances or frustrations. By offering constructive feedback in a professional and respectful manner, I demonstrate my commitment to the organization's success even as I move on to new opportunities.

Ultimately, quitting a job without burning bridges requires a combination of professionalism, communication skills, and emotional intelligence. By giving notice, communicating effectively, completing outstanding tasks, maintaining positive relationships, and providing constructive feedback, I can ensure that my departure is viewed as a positive step forward for both me and the organization.

CHAPTER 3: FIND YOUR PASSION, NOT ANOTHER JOB

Finding your passion, not just another job, is a deeply personal journey that requires introspection, exploration, and perseverance. For me, the quest to discover my true passion has been a process of self-discovery, trial and error, and continual learning. It begins with a willingness to explore my interests, values, and strengths, and to identify the activities and pursuits that bring me joy and fulfillment.

One of the first steps in finding my passion is to reflect on my past experiences and identify moments of flow —the times when I have been fully immersed in an activity, lost track of time, and felt a sense of purpose and satisfaction. These moments serve as clues to my passions and can help guide me towards discovering what truly ignites my enthusiasm and drives me to excel.

In addition to reflecting on past experiences, I also make a conscious effort to try new things and step outside of my comfort zone. This might involve taking classes, volunteering, or pursuing hobbies and interests that I have always been curious about but never had the chance to explore. By embracing new experiences and pushing myself to try new things, I open myself up to unexpected passions and opportunities for growth.

As I explore my interests and passions, I pay attention to how they align with my values and long-term goals. Finding my passion is not just about pursuing something that brings me joy in the moment—it is about finding work that is meaningful, fulfilling, and aligned with my values and aspirations. By connecting my passions to my values and goals, I ensure that my pursuit of passion is not just a fleeting indulgence but a meaningful and purposeful endeavor.

Another important aspect of finding my passion is seeking inspiration and guidance from others who have walked a similar path. I seek out mentors, role models, and peers who are enthusiastic about their work and can offer insights, advice, and support as I navigate my own journey. Learning from the experiences of others can provide valuable perspective and encouragement, helping me stay motivated and focused on my goals.

In my quest to find my passion, I also remain open to serendipity and unexpected opportunities. Sometimes, passion finds us in the most unexpected places, and it is important to remain open-minded and flexible in our pursuits. I embrace curiosity and embrace the unknown, knowing that each new experience brings me one step closer to discovering my true passion.

As I continue to explore my interests and passions, I remind myself that finding my passion is not always a linear process. There may be setbacks, challenges, and moments of doubt along the way, but each obstacle is an opportunity for growth and self-discovery. I embrace the journey, knowing that the pursuit of passion is as much about the process as it is about the destination.

Ultimately, finding my passion is about following my heart, trusting my instincts, and staying true to myself. It is about embracing the things that light me up inside and pursuing them with courage, determination, and enthusiasm. By staying true to my passions and values, I can build a career and a life that brings me joy, fulfillment, and a sense of purpose.

Self-Discovery: Tools and exercises to find what you truly love

Self-discovery is a journey of exploration and introspection that allows us to uncover our true passions, values, and aspirations. As I embark on this journey, I recognize the importance of using tools and exercises to help me identify what I love to do. These tools and exercises provide structure and guidance, helping me delve deep into my interests, strengths, and desires to uncover my unique path forward.

One powerful tool for self-discovery is journaling. I set aside time each day to reflect on my thoughts, feelings, and experiences, jotting down any insights or observations that arise. Journaling allows me to explore my interests, values, and goals in a structured and introspective way, helping me gain clarity and perspective on what truly matters to me.

Another valuable exercise for self-discovery is creating a vision board. I gather images, words, and symbols that resonate with me and represent my goals, dreams, and aspirations. By visually representing my desires and intentions, I can gain insight into what truly inspires and motivates me, helping me identify the activities and pursuits that align with my passions and values.

In addition to journaling and vision boards, I also use self-assessment tools to gain a deeper understanding of my personality, strengths, and preferences. Tools such as the Myers-Briggs Type Indicator (MBTI), StrengthsFinder, and Enneagram can provide valuable insights into my unique qualities and characteristics, helping me identify potential career paths and activities that are well-suited to my strengths and preferences.

Mindfulness practices, such as meditation and yoga, also play a crucial role in my journey of self-discovery. These practices help me cultivate awareness, presence, and acceptance, allowing me to connect more deeply with myself and uncover my innermost desires and aspirations. By quieting the mind and tuning into my body, I can tap into my intuition and inner wisdom, guiding me towards what truly lights me up inside.

Furthermore, seeking out new experiences and pushing myself outside of my comfort zone is essential for self-discovery. I actively seek out opportunities to try new things, explore new interests, and meet new people, knowing that each new experience brings me one step closer to uncovering my true passions and purpose. Whether it is taking a class, traveling to a new destination, or volunteering for a cause I care about, I embrace the unknown and trust that each new experience will enrich my journey of self-discovery.

The Passion Economy: Understanding how to monetize your interests.

Understanding how to monetize my interests is a journey of exploration and creativity that requires a combination of self-awareness, strategic thinking, and entrepreneurial spirit. As I embark on this journey, I recognize that my interests and passions have the potential to not only bring me joy and fulfillment but also to generate income and create opportunities for financial independence and success.

The first step in monetizing my interests is to identify

what excites and motivates me. Whether it is a hobby, skill, or area of expertise, I take the time to explore my interests and passions, paying attention to the activities that bring me the most joy and satisfaction. By gaining clarity on what I love to do, I can begin to brainstorm potential ways to turn my passions into profit.

Once I have identified my interests, I assess their marketability and potential demand. I research existing products, services, and businesses in my niche, paying attention to trends, competition, and consumer preferences. By understanding the market landscape, I can identify gaps and opportunities where my unique skills and offerings can provide value and meet the needs of potential customers.

Next, I develop a plan for how to monetize my interests, considering my goals, resources, and constraints. This might involve launching a freelance business, creating, and selling digital products or courses, offering consulting services, or monetizing my content through platforms such as YouTube, Patreon, or Etsy. I consider factors such as pricing, distribution channels, marketing strategies, and scalability, ensuring that my plan is both feasible and sustainable in the long term.

As I execute my plan, I remain flexible and open to feedback, adjusting and refining as needed based on market dynamics and customer feedback. I actively seek out opportunities to gain experience and grow, investing in my skills and knowledge to improve the quality and value of my offerings. By continuously iterating and improving my products and services, I can increase their appeal and effectiveness in the marketplace.

In addition to generating revenue directly from my interests, I also explore opportunities to diversify my income streams and create multiple sources of revenue. This might involve pursuing affiliate marketing partnerships, licensing my content or intellectual property, or exploring passive income opportunities such as investing in stocks, real estate, or digital assets. By diversifying my income streams, I can mitigate risk and create more stability and resilience in my financial situation.

As I navigate the process of monetizing my interests, I prioritize building relationships and fostering a community around my brand and offerings. I engage with my audience authentically, providing value, inspiration, and support, and seeking to create meaningful connections that go beyond transactional exchanges. By building trust and loyalty with my audience, I can cultivate a loyal customer base and create opportunities for repeat business and referrals.

Moreover, I leverage technology and digital platforms to amplify my reach and maximize my impact. I invest in building a strong online presence through social media, blogging, email marketing, and other digital channels, using these tools to connect with a global audience and expand my reach far beyond geographic boundaries. By harnessing the power of technology, I can scale my business and reach new heights of success.

Throughout the process of monetizing my interests, I remain committed to staying true to myself and my values. I prioritize passion, purpose, and integrity in all my endeavors, ensuring that my business reflects my authentic self and serves a greater purpose beyond just making money. By aligning my interests with my values, I can create a business that brings me not only financial success but also personal fulfillment and meaning.

Understanding how to monetize my interests is a journey of self-discovery, creativity, and entrepreneurship. By identifying my passions, assessing market opportunities, developing a strategic plan, and executing with purpose and integrity, I can turn my interests into profitable ventures that bring me joy, fulfillment, and financial independence. With dedication, perseverance, and a willingness to learn and adapt, I can create a thriving business that allows me to live life on my own terms and pursue my dreams with passion and enthusiasm.

Aligning Values and Work: Making sure your new path resonates with your personal values

Aligning my values with my work is a fundamental aspect of my professional life. The first step I take is to clearly identify my core values. This involves deep introspection to understand what drives me and what I stand for. For example, values such as integrity, creativity, and making a positive impact on society are central to who I am. By having a clear understanding of these values, I can make decisions that align with them and avoid compromising on what matters most to me.

When choosing a job or a project, I carefully assess whether the organization's mission and culture resonate with my values. I look for companies that prioritize ethical practices, encourage innovation, and contribute positively to the community. During interviews and research, I ask questions and seek information about the company's values and how they implement them in their operations. This alignment ensures that I am part of an environment where my values are respected and promoted.

In my daily work, I make a conscious effort to integrate my values into my actions and decisions. For instance, if I value integrity, I ensure that my work is honest and transparent, even when faced with challenges. If creativity is important to me, I seek opportunities to think creatively and propose innovative solutions. By embedding my values into my daily tasks, I not only stay true to myself but also enhance my job satisfaction and effectiveness.

Collaboration with colleagues is another area where aligning values is crucial. I strive to build relationships based on mutual respect and shared values. This involves open communication about what is important to me and understanding what drives my teammates. By creating a value-aligned team environment, we can work more cohesively and support each other in achieving both personal and collective goals. This constructive interaction enhances our productivity and creates a positive workplace culture.

When faced with ethical dilemmas or complex decisions at work, I use my values as a compass to navigate these challenges. I take time to reflect on the potential outcomes and ensure that my choices align with my principles. This might mean advocating for fair practices, standing up against unethical behavior, or making decisions that prioritize long-term benefits over short-term gains. By using my values as a guide, I maintain my integrity and contribute to a more ethical workplace.

Continuous self-reflection and feedback are essential in maintaining alignment between my values and work. I regularly evaluate whether my current role and activities still align with my core values. Seeking feedback from colleagues and mentors helps me identify areas for improvement and ensures that I am on the right path. This ongoing process of reflection and adjustment keeps me grounded and aligned with my values.

Ultimately, aligning my values with my work leads to a more fulfilling and meaningful career. When my professional life reflects what I honestly believe in, I experience greater satisfaction and motivation. This alignment not only benefits me personally but also enhances my contributions to my organization and society. By staying true to my values, I create a positive impact and build a career of which I am proud.

Making sure your path resonates with your personal values

When embarking on a new path, ensuring that it resonates with my personal values is essential for my sense of fulfillment and success. First, I begin with self-reflection. I take time to understand my core values and beliefs. This involves considering what truly matters to me, such as integrity, creativity, and helping others. By understanding my values, I can make more informed decisions about the direction I want to take.

Next, I set clear, value-aligned goals. I define what I want to achieve in a way that reflects my values. For instance, if one of my values is to make a positive impact, I set goals that focus on social entrepreneurship or community service. This alignment ensures that my efforts are not just about personal gain but also about contributing to something greater than myself.

I also seek out mentors and role models who embody similar values. Learning from individuals who share my values provides guidance and inspiration. Their experiences and advice can help me navigate challenges while staying true to my principles. By surrounding myself with value-driven people, I reinforce my commitment to my own values.

When evaluating opportunities, I perform a values check. I assess whether potential projects, partnerships, or roles align with my values. This involves asking myself critical questions about the ethical implications and the long-term impact of these opportunities. If something does not resonate with my values, I am willing to walk away, knowing that staying true to myself is more important.

In my daily activities, I practice mindfulness to stay connected to my values. I regularly check in with myself to ensure that my actions and decisions reflect what I stand for. This might mean taking a moment each day to reflect on whether my work and interactions are in harmony with my values. Mindfulness helps me stay grounded and authentic.

Transparency and communication are also crucial. I strive to be open about my values with colleagues, clients, and partners. By clearly expressing my values and expectations, I create an environment where mutual respect and understanding can flourish. This openness builds trust and ensures that everyone is on the same page.

I actively seek feedback from others to ensure I am living my values. Constructive feedback helps me identify areas where I might be straying from my principles or where I can improve. By being receptive to feedback, I can make necessary adjustments and continue to grow in a way that aligns with my values.

To maintain alignment, I set aside time for regular self-assessment. Periodically, I review my goals, actions, and decisions to ensure they still align with my values. This process helps me stay on track and adjust as needed. It is a way of reaffirming my commitment to living a value-driven life.

Lastly, I celebrate my achievements and milestones that reflect my values. Recognizing and celebrating these moments reinforces the importance of staying true to my principles. It also provides motivation to continue pursuing a path that resonates deeply with who I am. By celebrating these successes, I reinforce the positive impact of living according to my values.

CHAPTER 4: THE FREELANCER'S PLAYBOOK

Freelancing Basics: How to start freelancing in your field

Starting freelancing in my field was a crucial decision, and I knew I needed a structured approach to ensure success. First, I identified my specific skills and strengths. Understanding what I excel at and what services I could offer was crucial. I took inventory of my professional experiences, the projects I had worked on, and the feedback I had received. This helped me pinpoint the areas where I could provide the most value to potential clients.

Once I had a clear understanding of my skills, I began researching the market. I looked at what other freelancers in my field were offering, their rates, and how they positioned themselves. This market research provided insights into demand, pricing strategies, and potential gaps I could fill. I also joined online communities and forums where freelancers discussed their experiences and challenges. This helped me gain a realistic understanding of the freelance landscape.

With a solid understanding of the market, I created a portfolio displaying my work. This portfolio included detailed descriptions of past projects, results achieved, and testimonials from clients or colleagues. I ensured that my portfolio was visually appealing and easy to navigate, highlighting my best work. Having a professional and comprehensive portfolio was essential for attracting potential clients and demonstrating my capabilities.

Next, I established an online presence. I created a professional website that included my portfolio, a description of my services, and a blog where I shared insights related to my field. I also set up profiles on relevant freelancing platforms and social media. This online presence made it easier for potential clients to find me and learn about my expertise. It also allowed me to network with other professionals and stay updated on industry trends.

Networking played a crucial role in starting my freelancing journey. I reached out to former colleagues, attended industry events, and joined professional groups. By connecting with people in my field, I was able to spread the word about my freelancing services. Networking helped me get referrals and find opportunities that I might not have encountered otherwise. It also provided support and advice from others who had successfully transitioned to freelancing.

To manage my freelancing business effectively, I set up systems and processes. I created templates for proposals, contracts, and invoices to streamline administrative tasks. I also researched and invested in tools for project management, time tracking, and accounting. These systems helped me stay organized and professional, ensuring that I could focus on delivering high-quality work to my clients.

Marketing myself was another critical step. I developed a marketing plan that included content marketing, social media engagement, and email outreach. By sharing valuable content and engaging with my audience, I established myself as an expert in my field. I also reached out to potential clients directly, offering my services and explaining how I could help them achieve their goals. Consistent marketing efforts helped me build a steady stream of clients.

As I started taking on projects, I made it a priority to deliver exceptional work and build strong relationships with my clients. I communicated clearly and regularly, set realistic expectations, and met deadlines consistently. Providing excellent service led to positive reviews and repeat business, which are vital for a successful freelancing career. Happy clients often referred me to others, helping me expand my network and client base.

Finally, I continuously sought feedback and adapted my approach. Freelancing is dynamic, and I needed to stay flexible and responsive to changes in the market and client needs. I regularly reviewed my performance, sought feedback from clients, and made adjustments to improve my services. This commitment to growth and improvement helped me stay competitive and thrive as a freelancer in my field.

Building a Client Base: Networking and finding your first clients.

Building a client base and finding my first clients was a critical step in launching your freelancing career. Start by leveraging an existing network. I reached out to former colleagues, friends, and acquaintances to let them know about my new venture. By tapping into my existing connections, I was able to get the word out quickly and gain initial support. This network often provided valuable referrals, which led to my first few projects.

To expand my reach beyond my immediate network, join professional associations and attended industry events. These venues provided opportunities to meet potential clients and other freelancers. I made a point to introduce myself, exchange contact information, and follow up with people I met. By actively participating in these events, I built relationships and increased my visibility within my industry.

Online platforms were another essential tool for

finding clients. Create profiles on popular freelancing websites like Upwork, Fiverr, and LinkedIn. I carefully crafted these profiles to highlight my skills, experience, and the services I offered. I also included my portfolio and client testimonials to build credibility. These platforms made it easier for clients searching for my expertise to find and hire me.

Networking was not just about attending events or joining platforms; it was also about providing value. Start sharing your knowledge and insights through blog posts, social media updates, and participation in online forums. By consistently contributing valuable content, I positioned myself as an expert in my field. This not only attracted potential clients but also fostered trust and credibility.

Cold outreach was another strategy I employed. I researched companies and individuals who might need my services and reached out to them directly. I crafted personalized emails explaining how my skills could benefit their business and included a link to my portfolio. While this approach required persistence and many follow-ups, it eventually led to securing my first clients.

Utilize referral programs to encourage my existing clients to recommend me to others. I offered incentives, such as discounts on future projects, for clients who referred new business to me. This approach leveraged the trust and satisfaction of my current clients to help expand my client base organically. Word-of-mouth referrals became a powerful tool in building my reputation and attracting new clients.

Building strong relationships with my clients was crucial for retaining them and generating referrals. I focused on excellent communication, delivering high-quality work, and exceeding expectations. By understanding their needs and providing solutions that aligned with their goals, I built trust and long-term partnerships. Satisfied clients were more likely to return and recommend my services to others.

To continuously grow my client base, I maintained a proactive approach to networking. I regularly attended industry conferences, workshops, and webinars to meet new people and stay updated on industry trends. I also joined online communities related to my field, where I could connect with potential clients and other freelancers. This ongoing networking effort ensured that I was always expanding my reach and finding new opportunities.

I always sought feedback from my clients to improve my services. After completing projects, I asked for their honest opinions on what went well and where I could improve. This feedback helped me refine my processes and better meet client expectations. It also showed clients that I was committed to delivering the best possible service, which further strengthened our relationship and led to more referrals and repeat business.

Managing Freelance Life: Tips for staying productive and organized.

Staying productive and organized is essential for managing my freelancing business effectively. One of the most crucial strategies I employ is setting clear goals. I start each day, week, and month with specific, measurable objectives. By breaking down larger projects into smaller tasks, I can focus on achieving manageable milestones. This not only keeps me on track but also provides a sense of accomplishment as I complete each task.

Time management is another key factor in maintaining productivity. I use tools like calendars and scheduling apps to plan my days. Allocating specific time blocks for different tasks helps me stay focused and reduces the risk of procrastination. I also make sure to include breaks in my schedule to avoid burnout. By managing my time effectively, I ensure that I make the most of my working hours.

Creating a dedicated workspace is essential for maintaining organization and productivity. I have set up a home office that is free from distractions and equipped with everything I need to work efficiently. This physical separation between work and personal life helps me switch into a professional mindset when I enter my workspace. A well-organized and clutter-free environment boosts my concentration and efficiency.

To-do lists are indispensable for keeping track of my tasks and priorities. Each morning, I write a list of tasks I need to complete that day. I prioritize these tasks based on urgency and importance, ensuring that I tackle the most critical ones first. This practice helps me stay organized and ensures that I do not overlook any important deadlines or commitments.

I also leverage technology to stay organized. Project management tools like Trello or Asana help me keep track of multiple projects and deadlines. These platforms allow me to create task boards, set due dates, and monitor progress. Using these tools ensures that I have a clear overview of my workload and can easily adjust plans as needed.

Maintaining a healthy work-life balance is crucial for long-term productivity. I set boundaries for my work hours and make sure to take time off to recharge. This balance prevents burnout and keeps me motivated. By scheduling time for hobbies, exercise, and social activities, I maintain my overall well-being, which in turn enhances my productivity when I am working.

Regularly reviewing my progress and processes helps me stay productive. I take time at the end of each week to reflect on what I achieved and what could be improved. This reflection allows me to identify any inefficiencies or distractions and make necessary adjustments. Continuous improvement ensures that I am always optimizing my workflow and staying productive.

Effective communication is also vital for staying organized, especially when collaborating with clients and collaborators. I make sure to keep clear and open lines of communication, using tools like email, instant messaging, and video calls. Regular updates and check-ins help prevent misunderstandings and keep everyone on the same page. Clear communication saves time and ensures that projects run smoothly.

Lastly, I practice self-discipline and stay committed to my routines and schedules. It is easy to get distracted or put off tasks, but by staying disciplined and sticking to my plans, I maintain a consistent level of productivity. This commitment to my routines builds good habits over time, making it easier to stay organized and productive overall.

CHAPTER 5: ENTREPRENEURIAL MINDSET

Thinking Like a Boss: Shifting from employee to entrepreneur mindset

Shifting from an employee mindset to an entrepreneur mindset was a transformative experience for me. One of the first changes I made was taking full ownership of my work and decisions. As an employee, I was used to following directives and working within defined parameters. However, as an entrepreneur, I realized that every decision, success, and failure was entirely my responsibility. This sense of ownership empowered me to be more initiative-taking and accountable in all aspects of my business.

Another significant shift was embracing risk and uncertainty. In a traditional job, there is often a sense of security and predictability. Entrepreneurship, on the other hand, involves navigating unknown territories and taking calculated risks. I learned to view challenges as opportunities for growth and innovation. This mindset helped me to be more resilient and adaptable in the face of setbacks, knowing that each failure was a steppingstone toward success.

Thinking like a boss also meant developing a strategic vision for my business. As an employee, my focus was primarily on completing tasks and meeting short-term goals. As an entrepreneur, I needed to think long-term and create a sharp vision and mission for my business. This involved setting ambitious goals, planning, and continuously evaluating and adjusting my strategies to align with my vision. Having a strategic outlook kept me motivated and focused on the bigger picture.

Time management became crucial as I shifted to an entrepreneurial mindset. Unlike a typical job with fixed hours, running a business required me to manage my time efficiently and prioritize tasks effectively. I started using tools and techniques to plan my days, set goals, and track my progress. This disciplined approach to time management ensured that I stayed productive and balanced multiple responsibilities without feeling overwhelmed.

Networking and building relationships took on a new level of importance. As an employee, my network was limited to my colleagues and immediate industry contacts. As an entrepreneur, I needed to actively expand my network to include clients, partners, mentors, and other entrepreneurs. Building strong relationships helped me access valuable resources, gain insights, and create opportunities for collaboration.

Networking became a vital component of growing my business and achieving long-term success.

Economic management was another area where my mindset needed to shift. In a regular job, I received a steady paycheck and had limited involvement in the financial aspects of the company. As an entrepreneur, I had to manage all financial matters, from budgeting and accounting to investing in growth opportunities. I learned to be diligent about tracking expenses, forecasting revenue, and making informed financial decisions. This financial acumen was essential for sustaining and scaling my business.

Self-motivation and discipline became critical in my new role. Without a manager to provide direction and oversight, I had to rely on my own drive and determination to stay on course. I developed routines and habits that fostered productivity and kept me focused on my goals. This self-discipline helped me maintain momentum, even during challenging times, and ensured that I consistently worked towards achieving my business objectives.

Innovation and creativity flourished as I embraced the entrepreneurial mindset. I had the freedom to experiment with current ideas, explore different approaches, and take bold steps to differentiate my business. This creative freedom was both exhilarating and essential for staying competitive in the market. By fostering a culture of innovation, I could continuously improve my products and services, providing unique value to my clients.

Lastly, I learned the importance of continuous learning and personal development. The entrepreneurial journey is dynamic and constantly evolving, requiring me to stay updated with industry trends, acquire new skills, and adapt to changes. I invested time in reading, attending workshops, and seeking mentorship to enhance my knowledge and capabilities. This commitment to lifelong learning ensured that I remained agile and well-equipped to navigate the challenges and opportunities of entrepreneurship.

Risk and Reward: Understanding and managing the risks of entrepreneurship

Understanding and managing the risks of entrepreneurship is crucial for long-term success. One of the first steps I took was identifying the specific risks associated with my business. These included financial risks, market risks, operational risks, and personal risks. By understanding these potential pitfalls, I could develop strategies to mitigate them. This initial risk assessment provided a clear picture of what could go wrong and helped me prepare accordingly.

Financial risk is the most significant concern for many entrepreneurs. To manage this, I created a detailed business plan and budget, outlining all potential expenses and revenue streams. I also set aside a financial cushion to cover unexpected costs. Diversifying my income sources, such as offering different services or products, helped reduce dependency on a single revenue stream. Regularly reviewing and adjusting my financial plans ensured that I remained financially stable and could adapt to changes in the market.

Market risks, such as changing consumer preferences or increased competition, required continuous monitoring and adaptation. I conducted regular market research to stay informed about industry trends and customer needs. This proactive approach allowed me to pivot my business strategies when necessary, ensuring that I remained relevant and competitive. Additionally, I sought feedback from clients and made improvements based on their suggestions, which helped me stay aligned with market demands.

Operational risks, including inefficiencies and disruptions in the supply chain, were another area of focus. I implemented robust processes and systems to ensure smooth operations. This included using project management tools, maintaining clear communication channels, and establishing contingency plans for potential disruptions. By optimizing operations, I could minimize delays and maintain high-quality service for my clients.

Personal risks, such as burnout and work-life balance, were equally important to address. Running a business can be demanding, and it is easy to neglect personal well-being. I made a conscious effort to set boundaries between work and personal life, ensuring I took time to recharge and avoid burnout. Regular exercise, hobbies, and spending time with family and friends helped me maintain a healthy balance. Taking care of my well-being was essential for sustaining my productivity and motivation.

Insurance played a critical role in managing risks. I researched and obtained several types of insurance, such as liability insurance, property insurance, and health insurance. These policies provided a safety net, protecting my business and personal assets from unforeseen events. Having adequate insurance coverage gave me peace of mind and allowed me to focus on growing my business without constant worry about potential setbacks.

Building a dedicated support network was another key strategy for managing risks. I connected with mentors, joined professional associations, and participated in networking events. These connections provided valuable advice, support, and resources. Surrounding myself with experienced entrepreneurs and industry experts helped me navigate challenges more effectively and make informed decisions. This support network was invaluable in reducing the feeling of isolation and providing practical solutions to problems.

Continuous learning and staying updated with industry developments helped mitigate risks related to knowledge gaps. I regularly attended workshops, webinars, and conferences to enhance my skills and knowledge. Reading industry publications and staying informed about regulatory changes ensured that I remained compliant and competitive. This commitment to learning enabled me to anticipate changes and adapt my business strategies accordingly.

Lastly, maintaining flexibility and adaptability was crucial in managing entrepreneurial risks. I embraced change and remained open to innovative ideas and opportunities. This mindset allowed me to pivot quickly when faced with challenges or new market trends. Being adaptable meant that I could turn potential threats into opportunities for growth. By staying flexible, I ensured that my business could navigate the uncertainties of the entrepreneurial journey and continue to thrive.

Innovation and Creativity: Leveraging your unique ideas

Leveraging my unique ideas has been fundamental to distinguishing my business in a competitive market. The first step I took was cultivating a mindset of creativity and innovation. I encouraged myself to think freely and not be afraid to challenge the status quo.

By fostering an environment where new ideas were welcomed and explored, I was able to generate concepts that were not only unique but also had the potential to create significant value for my clients and my business.

Understanding the importance of my unique value proposition (UVP) was crucial. I focused on identifying what set my ideas apart from others in the market. This involved analyzing my strengths, the specific needs of my target audience, and how my ideas could address those needs in a novel way. By clearly articulating my UVP, I was able to effectively communicate the distinct benefits of my ideas to potential clients and stakeholders, making my business more attractive and competitive.

To refine and validate my unique ideas, I actively sought feedback from a diverse group of people, including mentors, colleagues, and potential customers. This feedback provided valuable insights into how my ideas could be improved and whether they resonated with my target audience. By being open to constructive criticism and making necessary adjustments, I ensured that my ideas were both innovative and practical, increasing their likelihood of success.

Prototyping and testing were essential steps in bringing my unique ideas to life. I created small-scale versions of my concepts and evaluated them in real-world scenarios. This allowed me to identify potential issues and gather data on their effectiveness. By iterating on these prototypes based on test results, I could refine my ideas and ensure they were ready for broader implementation. This approach minimized risks and maximized the potential for successful execution.

Networking and collaboration played a significant role in leveraging my unique ideas. I connected with other professionals and entrepreneurs who shared my passion for innovation. These collaborations often led to new perspectives and opportunities to enhance my ideas. By working with others who brought different skills and insights to the table, I was able to expand on my concepts and create more comprehensive solutions that appealed to a wider audience.

Marketing my unique ideas effectively was another critical step. I developed a robust marketing strategy that highlighted the distinct features and benefits of my ideas. This included creating engaging content, leveraging social media, and utilizing targeted advertising to reach my audience. By consistently communicating the unique aspects of my ideas, I was able to build brand recognition and attract customers who valued innovation and originality.

Protecting my intellectual property was also essential. I took steps to safeguard my unique ideas through patents, trademarks, and copyrights where applicable. This protection ensured that my innovations were legally recognized as my own, preventing others from copying or profiting from my work without permission. By securing my intellectual property, I could confidently share my ideas with the world, knowing they were protected.

Continuous improvement and staying ahead of trends were vital to maintaining the uniqueness of my ideas. I kept a close eye on industry developments and emerging technologies, always looking for ways to enhance and evolve my concepts. By staying driven and adaptable, I ensured that my ideas remained relevant and innovative. This commitment to ongoing innovation helped me sustain a competitive advantage and consistently offer fresh, valuable solutions to my clients.

Lastly, I embraced a mindset of resilience and persistence. Bringing unique ideas to fruition often involves overcoming numerous challenges and setbacks. I learned to stay motivated and focused on my vision, even when faced with obstacles. By maintaining a cheerful outlook and a strong belief in the value of my ideas, I was able to navigate difficulties and continue pushing forward. This resilience was key to turning my unique ideas into successful ventures.

CHAPTER 6: SIDE HUSTLES TO MAIN HUSTLES

Turning my side hustle into my main hustle was a transformative journey that required careful planning and dedication. The first step I took was evaluating the viability of my side hustle. I analyzed its profitability, market demand, and growth potential. This involved looking at my financial records, customer feedback, and industry trends. By understanding the strengths and weaknesses of my side hustle, I could make an informed decision about whether it was feasible to scale it into a full-time business.

Once I determined that my side hustle had the potential to become my main hustle, I created a detailed business plan. This plan outlined my goals, strategies, and the steps needed to transition from part-time to full-time. It included financial projections, marketing strategies, and operational plans. Having a clear roadmap helped me stay focused and organized, ensuring that I could manage the transition smoothly and effectively.

Financial stability was a crucial consideration. I made sure to save enough money to cover my living expenses for several months before making the switch. This financial cushion gave me the confidence to take the leap without the immediate pressure of generating income. Additionally, I sought ways to reduce my expenses and increase my savings during the transition period. This preparation was essential for mitigating the financial risks associated with moving to a full-time business.

Building a strong client base was another critical step. While my side hustle was still part-time, I focused on expanding my network and attracting more clients. I leveraged social media, attended industry events, and utilized word-of-mouth referrals to increase my visibility and reach. By establishing a solid client base before going full-time, I ensured that I had a steady stream of income and a foundation to build upon.

Time management became even more important during this transition. Balancing my side hustle with my full-time job required careful planning and discipline. I used tools like calendars and task lists to prioritize my tasks and manage my time effectively. Once I transitioned to full-time, these time management skills helped me stay productive and focused on growing my business. I also established a routine that allowed me to maintain a healthy work-life balance, which was crucial for long-term success.

Investing in professional development was another key strategy. I took courses, attended workshops, and read extensively to enhance my skills and knowledge. This continuous learning helped me stay competitive and adapt to industry changes. By improving my expertise, I could offer higher-quality services to my clients and differentiate my business from competitors. Investing in myself was one of the best ways to ensure the growth and success of my main hustle.

Marketing played a significant role in scaling my side hustle. I developed a comprehensive marketing plan that included digital marketing, content creation, and social media engagement. By consistently promoting my business and engaging with my audience, I built a strong brand presence and attracted more clients. Effective marketing helped me generate more leads and convert them into loyal customers, driving the growth of my main hustle.

Collaboration and networking continued to be important as I transitioned to a full-time business. I joined professional associations, participated in industry forums, and connected with other entrepreneurs. These relationships provided valuable insights, support, and opportunities for collaboration. Networking helped me stay informed about industry trends and best practices, and it opened doors to new business opportunities. Surrounding myself with a supportive community was vital for my growth and success.

Lastly, I maintained a resilient and adaptable mindset throughout the transition. Turning a side hustle into a main hustle comes with its challenges and uncertainties. I faced setbacks and obstacles, but I remained committed to my vision and goals. By staying adaptable, I could pivot my strategies when needed and find creative solutions to problems. This resilience was key to navigating the difficulties of entrepreneurship and achieving my goal of making my side hustle my main hustle.

Starting Small: How to begin with a side hustle.

Starting a side hustle is an exciting journey that offers the opportunity to pursue passions, explore new interests, and generate additional income. The first step in beginning a side hustle is identifying your interests, skills, and expertise. Consider what activities or hobbies you enjoy and excel at, as well as any professional skills or knowledge you possess. This self-assessment will help you narrow down potential side hustle ideas that align with your strengths and interests.

Once you have identified your areas of focus, research potential side hustle opportunities within those niches. Explore different industries, markets, and business models to find opportunities that match your skills and interests. Look for gaps or unmet needs in the market that you could address with your side hustle.

Additionally, consider the feasibility of each idea in terms of time commitment, resources required, and potential income.

Validation is a crucial step in the process of starting a side hustle. Before investing time and resources into launching your side hustle, evaluate the viability of your idea. This could involve conducting market research, soliciting feedback from potential customers, or creating a minimum viable product (MVP) to gauge interest. Validation helps ensure that there is demand for your product or service and gives you valuable insights into how to refine and improve your offering.

Once you have validated your side hustle idea, it is time to create a plan for execution. Develop a clear vision and set specific goals for your side hustle, such as the amount of income you want to generate or the number of clients you want to acquire. Break down your goals into actionable steps and create a timeline for achieving them. Consider factors such as time commitment, budget, and resources needed to execute your plan effectively.

Establishing a strong online presence is essential for promoting your side hustle and reaching potential customers. Create a professional website or online portfolio that highlights your products or services, highlights your skills and experience, and provides contact information for potential clients. Utilize social media platforms and online marketplaces to further promote your side hustle and connect with your target audience. Consistent and strategic online marketing can help you attract clients and grow your side hustle over time.

Networking is another valuable tool for building your side hustle. Reach out to friends, family, and professional contacts to let them know about your side hustle and ask for their support. Attend networking events, join industry groups, and participate in online communities related to your niche to expand your network and connect with potential clients or collaborators. Building relationships and making connections can open doors to new opportunities and help you grow your side hustle more quickly.

Managing your time effectively is crucial when balancing a side hustle with other commitments such as a full-time job or family responsibilities. Create a schedule that allows you to dedicate focused time to your side hustle each week. Prioritize tasks and set deadlines to ensure that you make progress toward your goals. Be realistic about what you can accomplish within the time constraints of your other commitments, and do not be afraid to delegate or outsource tasks when necessary.

Consistency is key to success in building a side hustle. Dedicate regular time and effort to your side hustle, even when progress may seem slow, or setbacks occur. Stay motivated and focused on your long-term goals and celebrate small wins along the way. Over time, your consistent efforts will compound, and you will see the results of your hard work.

Finally, do not be afraid to evolve and adapt your side hustle as needed. Keep an open mind and be willing to experiment with the latest ideas, strategies, and approaches. Stay attuned to feedback from customers, market trends, and your own experiences, and be willing to amend your side hustle accordingly. Flexibility and adaptability are essential qualities for success as an entrepreneur, and embracing change will help you navigate the challenges and opportunities of building a side hustle.

Scaling Up: Transitioning from side hustle to full-time business

Transitioning from a side hustle to a full-time business is a significant step that requires careful planning, dedication, and strategic decision-making. The first consideration in this transition is assessing the viability of turning your side hustle into a full-time venture. Evaluate factors such as the demand for your product or service, your ability to generate sufficient income, and the scalability of your business model. If your side hustle has shown consistent growth and has the potential to support you financially, it may be time to consider making the transition.

Financial preparation is essential when transitioning from a side hustle to a full-time business. Calculate your expenses and determine how much income your business needs to generate to cover these costs. Establish a financial safety net by saving enough money to cover your living expenses for several months, as it may take time for your business to become profitable on a full-time basis. Having a financial cushion will provide peace of mind and stability as you make the transition.

Developing a solid business plan is crucial for guiding your transition to a full-time business. Update your existing business plan or create a new one that outlines your goals, strategies, and action steps for scaling your business. Define your target market, identify growth opportunities, and set specific milestones and timelines for achieving your objectives. A well-thought-out business plan will serve as a roadmap for navigating the transition and achieving long-term success.

One of the most significant challenges in transitioning from a side hustle to a full-time business is managing your time effectively. As your business demands increase, you may need to reassess your priorities and your schedule. Allocate dedicated time for essential tasks such as business development, client work, marketing, and administrative duties. Establishing routines and systems will help you stay organized and productive as you transition to full-time entrepreneurship.

Building a strong client base is essential for sustaining and growing your full-time business. Leverage your existing network and relationships to attract new clients and expand your reach. Invest in marketing and promotional activities to increase visibility and generate leads. Provide excellent customer service and deliver high-quality work to retain clients and encourage referrals. As your business grows, focus on building long-term relationships with clients to ensure ongoing success.

As you transition to full-time entrepreneurship, it is essential to invest in your professional development and skill-building. Continuously seek opportunities to expand your knowledge, improve your skills, and stay updated on industry trends. Take courses, attend workshops, and seek mentorship to enhance your expertise and capabilities. Investing in yourself will not only benefit your business but also position you for long-term growth and success.

Maintaining a healthy work-life balance is crucial when transitioning to full-time entrepreneurship. As the demands of your business increase, it is easy to become consumed by work and neglect other aspects of your life. Set boundaries around your work hours and prioritize self-care activities such as exercise, hobbies, and spending time with loved ones. Remember that achieving a balance between work and personal life is essential for your well-being and overall happiness.

Seeking support and guidance from mentors, peers, and other entrepreneurs can be invaluable as you transition to full-time entrepreneurship. Surround yourself with a supportive network of individuals who can offer advice, encouragement, and perspective. Join industry associations, attend networking events, and participate in mastermind groups to connect with like-minded professionals and share experiences. Building a staunch support network will provide valuable resources and help you navigate the challenges of entrepreneurship more effectively.

Finally, embrace the journey and remain adaptable as you transition from a side hustle to a full-time business. Be prepared to face challenges, setbacks, and uncertainties along the way. Stay focused on your goals, maintain a take-charge attitude, and be willing to learn from your experiences. Embracing change and staying resilient will enable you to overcome obstacles and achieve success as a full-time entrepreneur.

CHAPTER 7: BUILDING YOUR BRAND

Building your brand is a multifaceted process that involves shaping perceptions, creating a unique identity, and fostering meaningful connections with your audience. The foundation of building your brand lies in defining your brand identity. Start by clarifying your mission, values, and vision for your brand. What do you stand for? What sets you apart from your competitors? Your brand identity should be authentic and resonate with your target audience, forming the basis for all your branding efforts.

Visual branding is a key component of building your brand. Develop a cohesive visual identity that reflects your brand personality and values. This includes elements such as your logo, color palette, typography, and imagery. Consistency is key – ensure that your visual branding is applied consistently across all touchpoints, including your website, social media profiles, marketing materials, and products or packaging. A strong visual identity helps to create brand recognition and reinforces your brand message.

Another important aspect of building your brand

is crafting compelling brand messaging. Your brand messaging should clearly communicate who you are, what you do, and why it matters to your audience. Develop a brand voice that is authentic, relatable, and consistent with your brand identity. Use your brand messaging to tell your story, connect with your audience on an emotional level, and differentiate yourself from competitors. Effective brand messaging builds trust and loyalty with your audience.

Building a strong online presence is essential for modern brands. Create a professional website that serves as the central hub for your brand online. Optimize your website for search engines (SEO) to improve visibility and attract organic traffic. In addition to your website, establish a presence on social media platforms that are relevant to your target audience. Share engaging content, interact with your followers, and build relationships with your audience. An active and engaging online presence helps to increase brand awareness and drive customer engagement.

Consistently delivering high-quality products or services is crucial for building a strong brand reputation. Your brand reputation is built on the experiences and perceptions of your customers. Focus on providing exceptional value, exceeding customer expectations, and delivering a positive customer experience at every touchpoint. Encourage and solicit feedback from your customers and use their input to continually improve your products or services. A positive brand reputation builds trust and credibility with your audience and fosters customer loyalty.

Building partnerships and collaborations can also help to strengthen your brand and expand your reach. Identify complementary brands or influencers in your niche and explore opportunities for collaboration. Collaborations can take many forms, such as co-branded products, joint marketing campaigns, or cross-promotion on social media. By partnering with other brands or influencers, you can tap into their audience and leverage their credibility to enhance your own brand.

Effective storytelling is a powerful tool for building your brand and connecting with your audience on a deeper level. Use storytelling to share the journey behind your brand, highlight your values and mission, and show the impact you are making in the world. Incorporate storytelling into your marketing materials, website content, social media posts, and other brand communications. Authentic and compelling storytelling helps to humanize your brand, build emotional connections with your audience, and differentiate you from competitors.

Building a community around your brand can further strengthen brand loyalty and advocacy. Create opportunities for your audience to engage with your brand and connect with like-minded individuals.

This could include hosting events, facilitating online forums or groups, or organizing community-driven initiatives. Foster a sense of belonging and shared identity among your audience and empower them to become brand ambassadors who advocate for your brand and help spread the word to others.

Continually monitor and evaluate your brand performance to ensure that you are meeting your goals and resonating with your audience. Use analytics tools to track key metrics such as website traffic, social media engagement, customer satisfaction, and brand sentiment. Analyze this data regularly to identify areas for improvement and refine your branding strategies accordingly. Building your brand is an ongoing process that requires adaptability, creativity, and a commitment to delivering value to your audience.

Personal Branding: Crafting your image and message

Crafting your image and message is a vital aspect of building a strong, recognizable brand. The first step in this process is to define your brand's core values and mission. These foundational elements should guide every decision you make about your brand's image and messaging. Start by asking yourself what your brand stands for, what it aims to achieve, and how it wants to be perceived by your target audience. A clear understanding of these aspects will help you create an image and message that resonates with your customers and reflects your brand's identity.

Next, focus on developing a unique and consistent visual identity. This includes your logo, color scheme, typography, and overall design aesthetic. Your visual elements should align with your brand's values and mission, and they should be consistently applied across all platforms and materials. Consistency in visual identity helps build recognition and trust, making it easier for customers to remember and identify your brand. Invest in professional design services if necessary to ensure that your visuals are polished and effective.

Your brand's voice is another critical component of your image and message. The tone and style of your communication should reflect your brand's personality and appeal to your target audience. Whether your brand voice is professional, friendly, playful, or authoritative, it should be consistent across all channels, including your website, social media, email marketing, and customer service interactions. A strong, consistent brand voice helps to humanize your brand and build a connection with your audience.

Crafting compelling brand messaging involves telling your brand's story in a way that engages and inspires your audience. Your messaging should convey the unique value proposition of your brand, highlighting what sets you apart from competitors and why customers should choose you. Use storytelling techniques to share your brand's journey, mission, and impact. Authentic and relatable stories can create an emotional connection with your audience, making your brand more memorable and trustworthy.

To effectively communicate your message, you need to understand your target audience deeply. Conduct market research to identify their needs, preferences, and pain points. Tailor your message to address these aspects, showing how your brand can provide solutions and add value to their lives. Use language and imagery that resonates with your audience's values and aspirations. By speaking directly to your audience's concerns and desires, you can create a message that is both relevant and compelling.

Engagement is key to crafting a successful brand image and message. Interact with your audience on social media, respond to comments and messages, and create content that encourages participation. Use interactive elements like polls, quizzes, and contests to involve your audience and make them feel valued. By fostering a two-way conversation, you can build a loyal community around your brand and gain valuable insights into your customers' preferences and feedback.

Your online presence is a crucial platform for communicating your image and message. Ensure that your website is user-friendly, visually appealing, and aligned with your brand identity. Regularly update your content to keep it fresh and relevant. Utilize SEO strategies to improve your visibility and reach a broader audience. Your social media profiles should also reflect your brand's image and message, with consistent visuals and messaging across all platforms.

Monitoring and measuring the effectiveness of your image and message is essential for continuous improvement. Use analytics tools to track engagement, reach, and conversion rates. Pay attention to customer feedback and reviews to understand how your brand is perceived. This data can help you identify what is working and what needs adjustment. Regularly review and refine your strategy to ensure that your image and message remain effective and aligned with your brand's goals.

Stay true to your brand's identity and values. Authenticity is key to building a strong and lasting brand. Avoid the temptation to chase trends that do not align with your brand's core values. Instead, focus on delivering consistent value and maintaining the integrity of your brand. Over time, a genuine and well-crafted image and message will build trust and loyalty among your customers, driving long-term success for your brand.

Social media: Utilizing social platforms to grow your brand

Utilizing social platforms to grow your brand is an essential strategy in today's digital age. The first step is choosing the right platforms for your brand. Each social media platform caters to different demographics and content types, so it is crucial to understand where your target audience spends their time. For instance, Instagram and TikTok are great for reaching younger audiences with visual content, while LinkedIn is more suited for B2B marketing and professional content. By selecting the right platforms, you can focus your efforts on where they will have the most impact.

Once you have chosen your platforms, it is important to create a cohesive and recognizable brand presence across all of them. This involves maintaining consistency in your visual identity, such as using the same logo, color scheme, and typography. Your brand's voice should also be consistent, whether you are posting on Twitter, Facebook, or any other platform. Consistency helps build brand recognition and trust, making it easier for your audience to identify and connect with your brand.

Content creation is the heart of any social media strategy. To grow your brand, you need to produce high-quality, engaging content that resonates with your audience. This could include blog posts, videos, infographics, and more. It is important to mix several types of content to keep your audience engaged and cater to different preferences. Additionally, your content should align with your brand's values and message, providing value to your audience through education, entertainment, or inspiration.

Engaging with your audience is another critical aspect of using social platforms to grow your brand. Social media is not just a broadcasting tool but a space for two-way communication. Respond to comments, answer questions, and participate in conversations relevant to your industry. Showing that you listen and care about your audience's opinions builds a community around your brand and fosters loyalty. Engaged followers are more likely to become loyal customers and advocates for your brand.

Leveraging analytics and insights provided by social media platforms can enhance your strategy. Most platforms offer tools to track engagement, reach, and other key metrics. By regularly reviewing these analytics, you can gain insights into what type of content performs best, when your audience is most active, and how your campaigns are doing. This data-driven approach allows you to refine your strategy continuously and ensure that your efforts are aligned with your audience's preferences and behaviors.

Paid advertising on social media is another powerful way to grow your brand. Platforms like Facebook, Instagram, and LinkedIn offer advanced targeting options that allow you to reach specific demographics, interests, and behaviors. Investing in paid ads can increase your visibility, attract new followers, and drive traffic to your website. It is important to create compelling ad content and test different variations to see what resonates best with your audience. Monitor your ad performance closely and adjust your strategy based on the results.

Collaborating with influencers and other brands can also help expand your reach on social platforms. Influencers already have established audiences that trust their recommendations. Partnering with influencers who align with your brand can introduce your products or services to a wider audience and lend credibility to your brand. Similarly, collaborating with other brands for joint campaigns or content can provide mutual benefits and reach new potential customers.

Running social media contests and giveaways is an effective way to boost engagement and attract new followers. These activities generate excitement and encourage users to interact with your brand. Make sure the prizes are relevant to your audience and require actions that benefit your brand, such as following your page, tagging friends, or sharing your content. Contests and giveaways can create buzz around your brand and significantly increase your social media presence.

Staying updated with the latest trends and changes in social media algorithms is crucial. Social media is constantly evolving, and strategies that work today might not be effective tomorrow. Stay informed about new features, tools, and best practices by following industry blogs, attending webinars, and participating in relevant online communities. Being adaptable and willing to experiment with current trends can help you stay ahead of the competition and continuously grow your brand on social platforms.

Content is King: Creating valuable content that attracts an audience

Creating valuable content that attracts an audience is a critical aspect of successful brand-building and engagement. The first step in this process is understanding your audience. Conduct thorough research to identify their interests, pain points, and preferences. Create detailed buyer personas that represent your ideal customers, which will help guide your content creation. By knowing who you are speaking to, you can tailor your content to address their specific needs and provide solutions to their problems.

Once you have a clear understanding of your audience, focus on creating content that provides real value. This could be educational, entertaining, or inspiring content, depending on your audience's preferences. Valuable content answers questions, solves problems, or offers new insights that your audience can benefit from. For instance, if you are a fitness brand, you might create content that includes workout tips, healthy recipes, or motivational stories. The key is to make your audience feel that engaging with your content is worth their time.

Diversifying your content formats is essential to keep your audience engaged. People consume content in diverse ways, so offering a variety of formats can help you reach a broader audience. Blog posts, videos, infographics, podcasts, and social media posts are just a few examples. Videos are great for visual learners, while podcasts cater to those who prefer to listen on the go. Experiment with different formats to see what resonates most with your audience and mix them up to maintain interest.

Consistency is another crucial factor in attracting and retaining an audience. Develop a content calendar to plan and schedule your content in advance. This ensures that you post regularly, keeping your audience engaged and coming back for more. Consistent posting also signals to search engines and social media algorithms that your brand is active, which can improve your visibility and reach. However, consistency should not compromise quality; always prioritize creating high-quality content over quantity.

SEO (Search Engine Optimization) is an important consideration when creating valuable content. Use relevant keywords that your audience is likely to search for in your content to improve its visibility on search engines. Conduct keyword research to identify the terms and phrases that are most relevant to your audience and industry. Incorporate these keywords naturally into your content, including in titles, headings, and meta descriptions. Optimizing your content for SEO can increase organic traffic to your site and attract a larger audience.

Promoting your content effectively is essential for reaching a wider audience. Share your content across multiple channels, including your website, social media platforms, email newsletters, and relevant online communities. Tailor your promotional strategy to each platform to maximize its impact. For example, create eye-catching graphics for Instagram, engaging snippets for Twitter, and detailed posts for LinkedIn. Encouraging your audience to share your content can also amplify its reach.

Engaging with your audience is key to building a loyal following. Respond to comments, answer questions, and participate in conversations related to your content. Showing that you value and appreciate your audience's input fosters a sense of community and loyalty. Additionally, user-generated content, such as testimonials, reviews, and social media posts featuring your brand, can enhance your content strategy. Highlighting user-generated content shows appreciation and adds credibility to your brand.

Analyzing and measuring the performance of your content helps you understand what works and what does not. Use analytics tools to track metrics such as views, shares, comments, and conversion rates. This data provides insights into which types of content resonate most with your audience and which platforms are most effective. Regularly reviewing these metrics allows you to refine your content strategy, focusing on what generates the most engagement and value for your audience.

Always be open to feedback and willing to adapt. Content creation is an ongoing process that requires flexibility and a willingness to learn. Solicit feedback from your audience through surveys, comments, and direct interactions. Use this feedback to improve your content and better meet your audience's needs. Staying attuned to your audience's evolving preferences and continuously improving your content will help you maintain a strong, engaged audience over time.

CHAPTER 8: FINANCIAL FREEDOM

Budgeting for Independence: Managing your finances when you are your own boss.

Managing your finances effectively is crucial when you are your own boss. The first step is to establish a clear budget that outlines your expected income and expenses. Start by listing all your sources of income, such as client payments, sales, and other revenue streams. Then, itemize your expenses, including rent, utilities, supplies, marketing, and any other costs associated with running your business. Having a detailed budget helps you understand your financial situation and make informed decisions.

Separating your personal and business finances is essential for maintaining clarity and organization. Open a dedicated business bank account and use it exclusively for business transactions. This separation makes it easier to track business expenses, manage cash flow, and prepare for tax season. It also provides a clearer picture of your business's financial health, helping you make better financial decisions.

Keeping meticulous records of all financial transactions is another key aspect of managing your finances. Save receipts, invoices, and bank statements, and use accounting software to track your income and expenses. Regularly update your records to ensure accuracy and to make it easier to monitor your financial performance. Accurate record-keeping is crucial for budgeting, tax preparation, and financial planning.

Understanding your tax obligations is critical when you are self-employed. Depending on your location and the nature of your business, you may need to pay income tax, self-employment tax, and other business-related taxes. Consult with a tax professional to ensure you understand your obligations and to help you plan for tax payments. Set aside a portion of your income regularly to cover your tax liabilities, so you are not caught off guard when tax season arrives.

Building an emergency fund is essential for financial stability. As a self-employed individual, your income may fluctuate, and having a financial cushion can help you manage unexpected expenses or periods of lower income. Aim to save at least three to six months' worth of living expenses in an easily accessible account. This fund will provide peace of mind and financial security, allowing you to focus on growing your business without worrying about short-term financial shortfalls.

Investing in professional help can be a wise decision for managing your finances. Hiring an accountant or financial advisor can provide valuable insights and assistance with budgeting, tax planning, and financial strategy. Professionals can help you identify potential financial pitfalls, optimize your financial practices, and ensure compliance with tax regulations. While this involves an additional expense, the benefits often outweigh the costs by providing better monetary management and planning.

Monitoring your cash flow is crucial for maintaining a healthy financial position. Regularly review your cash flow statements to understand the inflow and outflow of money in your business. Positive cash flow ensures that you have enough funds to cover your expenses and invest in growth opportunities. If you notice cash flow issues, take dynamic steps to address them, such as adjusting your pricing, reducing expenses, or improving your invoicing and payment processes.

Planning for retirement is often overlooked by self-employed individuals, but it is a critical aspect of fiscal management. Without an employer-sponsored retirement plan, it is up to you to set aside funds for your future. Explore retirement savings options such as Individual Retirement Accounts (IRAs) or Solo 401(k) plans and contribute regularly. Planning for retirement ensures long-term financial security and allows you to build a nest egg for your later years.

Continuously educate yourself about financial management. Stay informed about best practices, new tools, and changes in tax laws that may affect your business. Attend workshops, read books, and consider online courses to enhance your financial literacy. The more knowledgeable you are about managing your finances, the better equipped you will be to make sound financial decisions and steer your business toward success.

Investment Strategies: Growing your wealth beyond a regular paycheck

Growing your wealth beyond a regular paycheck involves adopting an initiative-taking approach to personal finance and investing. The first step is to develop a comprehensive financial plan. This plan should include your short-term and long-term financial goals, such as buying a home, saving for retirement, or starting a business. By clearly defining your goals, you can create a roadmap for your financial journey and identify the strategies needed to achieve them.

Investing is one of the most effective ways to grow your wealth. Start by educating yourself about several types of investments, such as stocks, bonds, mutual funds, real estate, and ETFs (Exchange-Traded Funds). Diversify your investment portfolio to spread risk and increase potential returns. Consider working with a financial advisor to help you develop an investment strategy tailored to your risk tolerance and financial goals. Remember, the earlier you start investing, the more you can benefit from compound interest.

Another way to grow your wealth is by maximizing your earnings potential. This might involve negotiating a higher salary at your current job, seeking promotions, or switching to a higher-paying job. Additionally, consider furthering your education or acquiring new skills that are in demand in your industry. Certifications, advanced degrees, or specialized training can make you more valuable in the job market and lead to higher income opportunities.

Passive income streams can significantly boost your wealth over time. Explore opportunities to generate passive income, such as investing in rental properties, dividend-paying stocks, peer-to-peer lending, or creating digital products like e-books or online courses. Passive income requires an initial investment of time or money but can provide ongoing revenue with minimal effort once established. Diversifying your income sources reduces reliance on a single paycheck and enhances financial stability.

Saving and managing expenses are also critical components of wealth building. Create a budget to track your income and expenses and identify areas where you can cut costs. Automate your savings by setting up regular transfers to a high-yield savings account or investment account. Aim to save at least 20% of your income, but adjust this percentage based on your financial goals and circumstances. Living below your means allows you to save and invest more, accelerating your wealth-building efforts.

Leveraging tax-advantage accounts can further enhance your wealth. Contribute to retirement accounts like a 401(k) or IRA, which offer tax benefits such as tax-deferred growth or tax-free withdrawals in retirement. Take advantage of employer matching contributions if available, as this is free money that can significantly boost your retirement savings. Additionally, consider health savings accounts (HSAs) and other tax-advantaged accounts to maximize your tax efficiency.

Networking and building relationships can open doors to new financial opportunities. Connect with professionals in your industry, attend networking events, and join online communities related to your interests. These connections can lead to job opportunities, business partnerships, or investment advice that can help you grow your wealth. Surrounding yourself with financially savvy individuals can also provide inspiration and motivation to achieve your financial goals.

Continuous learning and staying informed about financial trends are essential for growing your wealth. Read books, listen to podcasts, and follow financial news to keep up with market developments and investment opportunities. Consider joining investment clubs or online forums where you can discuss strategies and share insights with others. Staying educated allows you to make informed decisions and adapt your financial strategies as needed.

Maintaining a long-term perspective is crucial for wealth building. Wealthy growth takes time and requires patience, discipline, and resilience. Avoid making impulsive financial decisions based on short-term market fluctuations or economic uncertainties. Stick to your financial plan, regularly review your progress, and adjust your strategies, as necessary. By staying focused on your long-term goals and consistently applying sound financial practices, you can achieve financial independence and grow your wealth beyond a regular paycheck.

Emergency Funds and Savings: Preparing for financial uncertainties

Preparing for financial uncertainties is an essential part of maintaining financial health and stability. The first step in this process is creating an emergency fund. This fund should cover at least three to six months' worth of living expenses and be easily accessible in a savings account or money market account. An emergency fund provides a financial cushion during unexpected events such as job loss, medical emergencies, or major repairs, ensuring you have the means to manage these situations without going into debt.

Diversifying your income streams is another effective way to prepare for financial uncertainties. Relying solely on a single paycheck can be risky, especially if your industry is prone to fluctuations. Explore side hustle, freelance work, or passive income opportunities such as investments, rental properties, or creating digital products. Having multiple sources of income not only provides additional financial security but also increases your overall earning potential.

Insurance is a critical component of financial preparedness. Evaluate your insurance coverage to ensure it adequately protects you and your family against potential risks. Health insurance, life insurance, disability insurance, and homeowners or renters' insurance are some of the key policies to consider. Adequate insurance coverage can prevent financial devastation in the event of illness, injury, or other unforeseen circumstances, providing peace of mind and financial stability.

Creating a detailed budget and sticking to it helps you manage your finances more effectively and prepare for uncertainties. Track your income and expenses, categorize your spending, and identify areas where you can cut costs or save more. A well-maintained budget ensures that you live within your means, allocate funds towards savings, and are better prepared to manage unexpected financial challenges. Regularly reviewing and adjusting your budget as needed helps you stay on track with your financial goals.

Reducing and managing debt is crucial when preparing for financial uncertainties. Elevated levels of debt can strain your finances, making it difficult to save and increasing your vulnerability during tough times. Focus on paying down high-interest debt, such as credit card balances, as quickly as possible. Consider consolidating or refinancing loans to lower your interest rates and monthly payments. By reducing your debt burden, you free up more resources for savings and investments, improving your overall financial resilience.

Investing in education and skills development can provide long-term financial security. Continuously improving your skills and knowledge makes you more valuable in the job market and increases your employability. Consider pursuing additional certifications, attending workshops, or taking online courses relevant to your field. Staying competitive and adaptable in your career can help you navigate economic downturns and job market shifts, ensuring a steady income even during uncertain times.

Building a strong network of professional and personal contacts can also help you prepare for financial uncertainties. Networking can lead to new job opportunities, business partnerships, or financial advice. Engage with industry peers, attend networking events, and join professional organizations to expand your connections. Having a supportive network can provide resources and support during challenging times, helping you recover and bounce back more quickly.

Regularly reviewing and adjusting your financial plan is essential for staying prepared. Life circumstances and economic conditions can change, affecting your financial situation. Periodically assess your financial goals, budget, savings, investments, and insurance coverage to ensure they remain aligned with your current needs and future aspirations. Being proactive and adaptable in your financial planning allows you to respond effectively to uncertainties and stay on track with your financial objectives.

Preserving a positive mindset and staying informed about financial matters can significantly enhance your ability to prepare for uncertainties. Stay updated on economic trends, financial news, and best practices for personal finance management. A bold approach to financial planning empowers you to make informed decisions, take control of your financial future, and navigate uncertainties with confidence. By being well-prepared, you can turn financial challenges into opportunities for growth and resilience.

CHAPTER 9: THE NETWORK EFFECT

Building Connections: Effective networking strategies

Building connections and developing effective networking strategies are crucial for personal and professional growth. The first step is to set clear networking goals. Understand what you want to achieve through networking, whether it is finding a new job, gaining industry insights, or forming business partnerships. Having specific goals helps you focus your efforts and measure your progress, making your networking activities more purposeful and effective.

Attending industry events and conferences is a valuable networking strategy. These gatherings provide opportunities to meet professionals in your field, learn about the latest trends, and gain new perspectives. When attending these events, come prepared with business cards, a clear introduction, and a few talking points about your background and interests. Engaging in conversations and showing genuine interest in others can help you establish meaningful connections.

Leveraging social media platforms like LinkedIn, X, and Facebook can significantly enhance your networking efforts. LinkedIn is a powerful tool for connecting with professionals, joining industry groups, and participating in discussions. Keep your profile updated, share relevant content, and actively engage with posts from others in your network. This not only increases your visibility but also demonstrates your expertise and commitment to your field.

Volunteering for industry-related activities or community events can also be an effective way to build connections. By contributing your time and skills, you can meet like-minded individuals and gain visibility within your community or industry. Volunteering shows your dedication and willingness to give back, which can leave a positive impression and open doors to new opportunities.

Joining professional organizations and associations provides access to a network of individuals with similar interests and career goals. These organizations often host events, workshops, and conferences that facilitate networking. Becoming an active member by participating in committees or taking on leadership roles can enhance your visibility and credibility within the organization, leading to more valuable connections.

Informational interviews are a targeted networking strategy that can yield significant benefits. Reach out to individuals whose careers or businesses you admire and request a brief meeting to learn more about their experiences and insights. These interviews not only provide valuable information but also help you establish a personal connection. Always express gratitude for their time and follow up with a thank-you note to leave a lasting positive impression.

Effective networking involves building and maintaining relationships over time. It is important to stay in touch with your connections by sending occasional updates, sharing relevant articles, or congratulating them on their achievements. Regular communication keeps you on their radar and reinforces your professional relationship. Remember that networking is a two-way street; offer your help and support when your connections need it.

Developing strong people skills is essential for successful networking. Active listening, empathy, and effective communication help you connect with others on a deeper level. Practice asking open-ended questions, showing genuine interest in the responses, and providing thoughtful feedback. Building rapport through these interactions can make your connections more meaningful and beneficial in the long run.

Be patient and persistent in your networking efforts. Building a robust professional network takes time and consistent effort. Not every interaction will lead to immediate results, but maintaining a motivated attitude and staying committed to your networking goals will pay off in the long term. Keep refining your strategies, expanding your network, and nurturing your relationships to create a supportive and valuable network that can help you achieve your personal and professional aspirations.

Mentorship and Guidance: Finding and leveraging mentors

Finding and leveraging mentors is a powerful strategy for personal and professional development. The first step in this process is identifying what you need in a mentor. Consider your career goals, the skills you want to develop, and the areas where you need guidance. By clearly understanding your needs, you can identify individuals who have the experience and knowledge to help you grow. Look for mentors who have achieved what you aspire to and who share your values and work ethic.

Once you have identified potential mentors, the next step is to approach them thoughtfully and respectfully. Start by researching their background and accomplishments to understand their journey. When you reach out, be clear about why you admire them and how you believe they can help you. Be concise and specific in your request for mentorship and express your willingness to learn and grow. Remember, many successful individuals are busy, so be respectful of their time.

Building a relationship with a mentor requires mutual respect and open communication. Regularly check in with your mentor, share your progress, and seek their advice on specific challenges or decisions. Be open to feedback and willing to implement their suggestions. A good mentor-mentee relationship is built on trust and honesty, so be transparent about your goals, struggles, and achievements. Show appreciation for their time and insights, and make sure the relationship is beneficial for both parties.

Leveraging your mentor's knowledge and experience can significantly accelerate your growth. Actively seek their guidance on career development, skill enhancement, and navigating industry challenges. Ask them to share their experiences, both successes and failures, and learn from their journey. Mentors can provide valuable perspectives that you might not have considered and can help you avoid common pitfalls. Apply their advice and insights to your own situation to achieve better results.

Networking is another area where mentors can be incredibly valuable. They can introduce you to their professional network, providing opportunities to connect with other influential individuals in your field. These connections can lead to new job opportunities, partnerships, or collaborations. When leveraging your mentor's network, be respectful and professional, understanding that their reputation is tied to your interactions. Building a strong network through your mentor can open many doors and enhance your career prospects.

In addition to career guidance, mentors can offer support and encouragement during challenging times. They can provide a sounding board for your ideas, help you navigate tough decisions, and offer reassurance when you face setbacks. This emotional support can be crucial for maintaining motivation and resilience. Knowing that someone experienced believes in your potential can boost your confidence and help you stay focused on your goals.

It is important to give back to your mentor as well. While you may not have the same level of experience, you can offer fresh perspectives, share your own knowledge, or assist them with projects or tasks. Showing that you value and appreciate their mentorship by being a dependable and engaged mentee strengthens the relationship. Additionally, expressing gratitude and recognizing their contributions can foster a positive and lasting mentorship.

Finding multiple mentors can provide a well-rounded support system. Different mentors can offer diverse perspectives and expertise in various areas of your life and career. For example, one mentor might help you with technical skills, while another offers guidance on leadership and personal development. By building a network of mentors, you can draw on a wide range of experiences and advice, making your development more comprehensive and robust.

As you benefit from mentorship, consider becoming a mentor yourself. Sharing your knowledge and experience with others not only helps them but also reinforces your own learning and growth. Mentoring others can provide a sense of fulfillment and purpose, and it helps you build leadership and communication skills. By giving back to the community and supporting the next generation of professionals, you contribute to a culture of continuous learning and development.

Collaborations and Partnerships: Working with others for mutual benefit

Working with others for mutual benefit is a foundational principle of successful relationships, both in personal and professional contexts. The first step in fostering these relationships is establishing clear and open communication. When working with others, it is essential to articulate your goals, expectations, and any constraints you might have. Similarly, take the time to understand the needs and objectives of your collaborators. Clear communication helps prevent misunderstandings and ensures that everyone is on the same page, creating a solid foundation for a productive partnership.

Building trust is another crucial element in working effectively with others. Trust is built over time through consistent actions, honesty, and reliability. By following through on your commitments, being transparent about your intentions, and respecting others' contributions, you can foster a sense of trust that makes collaboration smoother and more effective. Trust not only enhances cooperation but also encourages a more open exchange of ideas, as individuals feel secure in sharing their thoughts and feedback.

Identifying common goals and interests is vital for creating mutually beneficial relationships. When working with others, look for areas where your objectives align. This common ground serves as the basis for collaboration, ensuring that both parties are working towards a shared vision. Whether it is a business project, a community initiative, or a personal endeavor, aligning goals helps maintain focus and direction, making the collaboration more meaningful and effective.

Sharing resources and knowledge is an integral part of mutually beneficial relationships. When individuals bring their unique skills, experiences, and resources to the table, it creates a richer pool of assets that everyone can draw from. This sharing can lead to innovative solutions and improved outcomes that might not have been possible if working independently. Be generous with your expertise and open to learning from others, fostering a collaborative environment where everyone benefits.

Effective problem-solving often requires diverse perspectives and approaches. When working with others, leverage the diversity of thought and experience to tackle challenges more creatively and efficiently. Encourage brainstorming sessions where all ideas are considered and use the collective knowledge of the group to find the best solutions. By valuing and incorporating different viewpoints, you can enhance the quality of your decisions and outcomes.

Mutual respect is key to successful collaboration. Respect each other's time, opinions, and contributions. Acknowledge the efforts and achievements of your collaborators and provide constructive feedback that helps them grow. Creating an environment of mutual respect fosters a positive and productive atmosphere where everyone feels valued and motivated to contribute their best.

Flexibility and adaptability are important traits when working with others. Be open to new ideas and willing to adjust your plans as needed. Collaboration often involves compromise and the ability to pivot when circumstances change. Flexibility shows that you are considerate of others' perspectives and are committed to finding solutions that work for everyone involved. This adaptability can lead to more resilient and dynamic partnerships.

Celebrating successes together strengthens the bond between collaborators and reinforces the value of working together. Take the time to recognize and celebrate both small and large achievements. Whether it is a successful project completion, reaching a milestone, or simply a job well done, acknowledging these moments fosters a sense of camaraderie and shared accomplishment. Celebrations can also serve as a reminder of what you can achieve together, motivating everyone to continue striving for excellence.

Continuing long-term relationships beyond individual projects can lead to ongoing mutual benefits. Stay connected with your collaborators, check in on their progress, and look for future opportunities to work together. Building a network of trusted collaborators can provide support, resources, and opportunities over time. These long-term relationships are valuable assets that can enhance your personal and professional life, creating a cycle of mutual benefit and continuous growth.

CHAPTER 10: OVERCOMING SETBACKS

Handling Failure: Learning from mistakes and moving forward

Learning from your mistakes and moving forward is a crucial aspect of personal and professional growth. The first step in this process is acknowledging your mistakes without being overly critical of yourself. Everyone makes mistakes and recognizing them as part of the learning journey helps you approach them constructively. Accepting responsibility for your actions is essential for growth and prevents you from repeating the same errors.

Once you have acknowledged your mistake, take the time to analyze what went wrong. Reflect on the factors that led to the error, including your decision-making process, external circumstances, and any lapses in judgment or skill. Understanding the root cause of the mistake allows you to identify specific areas for improvement. This analysis should be thorough but balanced, focusing on learning rather than assigning blame.

Learning from your mistakes involves extracting valuable lessons and insights. Consider what you could have done differently and how you can apply these lessons to future situations. This might involve developing new skills, adjusting your strategies, or changing your approach to certain tasks. By transforming your mistakes into learning opportunities, you can turn setbacks into steppingstones for future success.

It is also important to seek feedback from others when you make a mistake. Colleagues, mentors, or supervisors can provide valuable perspectives that you might not have considered. Constructive feedback helps you gain a more comprehensive understanding of what went wrong and how to improve. Be open to their input and willing to make the necessary changes. Engaging in open dialogue about your mistakes fosters a culture of learning and growth.

Developing resilience is key to moving forward after making a mistake. Resilience involves maintaining and persevering despite setbacks. When you encounter difficulties, remind yourself that mistakes are part of the process and that each one brings you closer to your goals. Cultivating resilience helps you stay focused and motivated, enabling you to bounce back more quickly and effectively.

Creating a plan to address and prevent future mistakes is an essential step in the learning process. Based on your reflections and feedback, outline specific actions you will take to avoid similar errors in the future. This might include additional training, seeking advice before making critical decisions, or implementing new processes. Having a plan in place empowers you to move forward with confidence and reduces the likelihood of repeating past mistakes.

It is also beneficial to share your experiences and the lessons you have learned with others. By being open about your mistakes, you can help your colleagues avoid similar pitfalls and foster a collaborative environment where continuous improvement is valued. Sharing your journey demonstrates humility and a commitment to personal and team growth. It can also strengthen your relationships with others, as they see you as someone who is transparent and willing to learn.

Moving forward from mistakes requires a balance between learning from the past and focusing on the future. While it is important to reflect on and understand your errors, do not dwell on them to the point of hindering your progress. Use the insights gained to inform your actions and decisions moving forward but keep your focus on your goals and the steps needed to achieve them. This forward-thinking mindset helps you stay motivated and productive.

Practice self-compassion throughout this process. Being hard on yourself for making mistakes can lead to unnecessary stress and a negative self-image. Instead, treat yourself with the same kindness and understanding you would offer a friend in a similar situation. Recognize that making mistakes is a natural part of the learning process and an opportunity for growth. By maintaining a compassionate attitude towards yourself, you can more effectively learn from your mistakes and move forward with confidence and determination.

Stress Management: Techniques to stay sane during the entrepreneurial journey

Staying sane during the entrepreneurial journey is crucial for maintaining both mental health and business productivity. One of the most effective techniques is establishing a healthy work-life balance. As an entrepreneur, it can be tempting to immerse yourself completely in your work, but it is important to set boundaries between your personal and professional life. Designate specific times for work and stick to them, allowing yourself to fully disconnect and recharge outside of these hours. Prioritizing activities that bring you joy, and relaxation helps prevent burnout and keeps you mentally refreshed.

Regular physical activity is another essential technique for maintaining sanity. Exercise has numerous mental health benefits, including reducing stress, anxiety, and depression. Incorporate regular workouts into your routine, whether it is going for a run, attending a yoga class, or simply taking a walk during lunch breaks. Physical activity boosts your energy levels and enhances your mood, making it easier to tackle the challenges of entrepreneurship with a clear and focused mind.

Mindfulness and meditation practices can significantly enhance your mental well-being. These techniques help you stay present, reduce stress, and improve your ability to manage pressure. Start by dedicating a few minutes each day to mindfulness exercises or meditation. Apps like Headspace or Calm can guide you through these practices if you are new to them. Over time, mindfulness can increase your emotional resilience and provide a sense of calm amidst the chaos of running a business.

Creating a support network is vital for navigating the difficulties of entrepreneurship. Surround yourself with supportive friends, family, mentors, and fellow entrepreneurs who understand the challenges you face. Regularly connect with these individuals to share your experiences, seek advice, and gain different perspectives. A good support network can offer emotional support, practical advice, and motivation, helping you stay grounded and focused on your goals.

Setting realistic goals and expectations is crucial

for maintaining sanity. While ambition drives entrepreneurs, setting unattainable goals can lead to frustration and stress. Break down your long-term objectives into smaller, manageable tasks and celebrate each milestone achieved. This approach not only keeps you motivated but also provides a clear sense of progress, reducing the overwhelm that often accompanies large, undefined goals.

Time management techniques are essential for staying organized and reducing stress. Tools like to-do lists, calendars, and project management software can help you prioritize tasks and allocate your time efficiently. The Pomodoro Technique, which involves working in focused intervals followed by short breaks, can enhance productivity and prevent burnout. Effective time management ensures that you stay on top of your responsibilities without feeling overwhelmed.

Practicing self-care is fundamental to staying sane during the entrepreneurial journey. Allocate time for activities that nourish your body and mind, such as hobbies, reading, or spending time in nature. Ensure you get enough sleep, eat healthily, and stay hydrated. Self-care is not a luxury but a necessity for maintaining the mental and physical energy required to run a business successfully.

Learning to delegate and ask for help can significantly reduce your stress levels. As an entrepreneur, it is easy to fall into the trap of thinking you need to do everything yourself. Identify tasks that can be outsourced or delegated to others, whether it is hiring an assistant, using freelance services, or collaborating with business partners. Delegating allows you to focus on your strengths and the strategic aspects of your business, while also giving you more time to rest and recharge.

Maintaining a positive mindset and practicing gratitude can influence your mental health. Entrepreneurship is filled with highs and lows, and focusing on the positives helps you stay motivated and resilient. Start a gratitude journal, where you note down things you are thankful for each day. Reflecting on your achievements, no matter how small, and maintaining a hopeful outlook can make a significant difference in your overall well-being and ability to persevere through challenges.

Persistence Pays Off: Stories of perseverance and success after failure

Perseverance and success after failure are fundamental themes in the journey of many accomplished individuals. The first step to achieving success after failure is accepting that failure is a natural part of the process. Everyone encounters setbacks and understanding that these are not the end but rather opportunities for learning and growth is crucial. Embracing failure allows you to analyze what went wrong, learn from your mistakes, and develop strategies to avoid similar issues in the future.

A key aspect of perseverance is maintaining a positive mindset despite setbacks. It is essential to view failures not as reflections of your capabilities but as experiences that provide valuable lessons. Cultivating a positive outlook helps you stay motivated and focused on your goals. This attitude enables you to bounce back more quickly and keep moving forward with renewed energy and determination. Positive thinking can transform challenges into steppingstones on the path to success.

Setting realistic and achievable goals is another important strategy for persevering through failure. Break down your long-term objectives into smaller, manageable tasks that can be accomplished step-by-step. Celebrating small victories along the way keeps you motivated and provides a clear sense of progress. This approach helps prevent feelings of overwhelm and allows you to maintain steady momentum towards your ultimate goals.

Resilience plays a critical role in overcoming failure and achieving success. Resilience is the ability to adapt to challenges and recover from setbacks. Developing resilience involves building mental and emotional strength, which can be achieved through practices such as mindfulness, meditation, and regular physical exercise. Resilient individuals are better equipped to manage stress and are more likely to persevere in the face of adversity.

Seeking support from others is essential for maintaining perseverance after failure. Surround yourself with a network of supportive friends, family, mentors, and colleagues who can provide encouragement, advice, and perspective. Sharing your experiences and challenges with others can lighten your emotional load and offer new insights. A dedicated support network can help you stay grounded and motivated, making it easier to persevere through tough times.

Learning from your failures involves a thorough analysis of what went wrong and why. Reflect on the decisions and actions that led to the failure and consider what you could have done differently. This process of self-reflection is crucial for identifying areas for improvement and developing new strategies. By understanding the root causes of your failures, you can make informed changes and increase your chances of success in future endeavors.

Flexibility and adaptability are vital for persevering through failure and achieving success. Be willing to adjust your plans and strategies based on the lessons learned from your failures. Sometimes, the path to success may require taking a different approach or exploring new opportunities. Being adaptable allows you to respond effectively to changing circumstances and increases your ability to overcome obstacles.

Staying committed to your vision is essential for

long-term success. Perseverance means continuing to pursue your goals even when faced with setbacks and failures. Reaffirm your commitment to your vision by regularly revisiting your goals and reminding yourself of why you started. This sense of purpose can provide the motivation and drive needed to keep going, even when the journey becomes challenging.

Remember that success is often a marathon, not a sprint. Achieving significant goals and overcoming failures takes time, patience, and consistent effort. Stay focused on your long-term vision and be patient with yourself as you navigate the difficulties of the journey. Celebrate your progress, learn from your experiences, and keep moving forward with determination and resilience. By persevering through failure and having a positive approach, you can turn setbacks into steppingstones and achieve the success you desire.

CHAPTER 11: THE DIGITAL NOMAD LIFE

Remote Work Essentials: Tools and tips for working from anywhere

Working from anywhere is becoming increasingly common and offers the flexibility to balance work and personal life in new ways. However, to make the most of this freedom, it is essential to equip yourself with the right tools and strategies. The first and most crucial step is ensuring you have a reliable internet connection. High-speed internet is the backbone of remote work, enabling smooth video calls, quick file downloads, and efficient access to cloud-based applications. Consider having a backup plan, such as a portable Wi-Fi device or knowing the locations of local cafés and coworking spaces with reliable Wi-Fi, to avoid disruptions.

Equipping yourself with the right hardware is also vital. Invest in a high-quality laptop that meets your work needs in terms of processing power, storage, and portability. Accessories like a comfortable mouse, a laptop stand, and noise-canceling headphones can enhance your remote work setup. These tools not only increase productivity but also help maintain ergonomics, reducing strain from prolonged use. Additionally, having a reliable power bank or portable charger can be a lifesaver when working in locations where power outlets are not readily available.

Software tools are equally important for effective remote work. Cloud-based platforms like Google Workspace or Microsoft Office 365 allow you to create, store, and share documents seamlessly. Project management tools such as Trello, Asana, or Monday.com help you keep track of tasks and deadlines, ensuring you stay organized and productive. For communication, Slack and Microsoft Teams are popular choices for real-time collaboration with colleagues. These tools keep you connected and enable efficient teamwork regardless of physical location.

Maintaining a regular schedule is essential for productivity when working from anywhere. Establish a routine that includes set working hours, breaks, and time for personal activities. This helps create a sense of normalcy and discipline, ensuring that you remain focused and productive. Use digital calendars to schedule your tasks and meetings and set reminders to stay on track. Consistency in your routine helps manage time effectively and prevents work from spilling over into personal life.

Creating a dedicated workspace, even if temporary, can significantly enhance your focus and productivity.

Choose a quiet, comfortable spot where you can work without distractions. Personalize this space with items that boost your motivation and creativity, such as plants, artwork, or a comfortable chair. Having a defined workspace helps signal to your brain that it is time to work, fostering better concentration and efficiency.

When working from various locations, it is important to stay connected with your team. Regular check-ins through video calls or instant messaging keep everyone updated and aligned. Use collaborative tools to share progress and feedback and communicate any issues or delays. Building a strong remote team culture can involve virtual coffee breaks, team-building activities, and regular updates to maintain a sense of community and support.

Staying organized is crucial for remote work success. Develop a system for managing your files, whether through cloud storage solutions like Dropbox or Google Drive or through organizational tools like Evernote or Notion. Keeping your digital workspace tidy helps you find documents quickly and reduces stress. Regularly back up your important files to avoid data loss and ensure you can access your work from any device.

Self-care is essential when working from anywhere. Without the structure of a traditional office, it is easy to fall into the trap of working long hours without breaks. Schedule regular breaks to stretch, move around, and rest your eyes. Incorporate activities that promote well-being, such as exercise, meditation, or spending time outdoors. Maintaining a healthy work-life balance is key to sustaining productivity and avoiding burnout.

Finally, continuously refine your remote work skills. Stay updated with new tools and techniques that can enhance your productivity and efficiency. Join online communities or forums where remote workers share tips and experiences. Attend webinars or take courses on remote work best practices. By staying informed and adaptable, you can maximize the benefits of working from anywhere and maintain an elevated level of performance and satisfaction in your professional life.

Travel and Work: Balancing work with the digital nomad lifestyle

Balancing work with the digital nomad lifestyle is a rewarding but challenging endeavor that requires careful planning and disciplined execution. The allure of exploring new destinations while maintaining your professional responsibilities can be incredibly appealing, but it also demands a prominent level of organization and flexibility. The first step in achieving this balance is setting clear boundaries between work and leisure. Establish specific working hours and adhere to them as much as possible, even when you are in a different time zone or a new, exciting location. This structure helps ensure that work tasks are completed efficiently, leaving ample time to enjoy your surroundings.

Choosing the right location is crucial for a successful digital nomad lifestyle. Not all destinations are equally conducive to remote work. Look for places with reliable internet connectivity, accessible coworking spaces, and a stable power supply. Cities known for their digital nomad communities, such as Bali, Chiang Mai, or Lisbon, often have the necessary infrastructure and a supportive network of fellow remote workers. These environments can enhance productivity and provide a sense of community, reducing the isolation that sometimes accompanies remote work.

Efficient time management becomes even more critical when balancing work and travel. Utilize digital tools like calendars, task management apps, and time-tracking software to keep your schedule organized. The Pomodoro Technique, which involves working in focused intervals followed by short breaks, can help maintain productivity and prevent burnout. Prioritize tasks based on deadlines and importance and be mindful of time zone differences when scheduling meetings or communicating with clients and colleagues.

Maintaining a healthy work-life balance is essential for your well-being. The digital nomad lifestyle can blur the lines between work and leisure, leading to overwork and stress. Schedule regular breaks and allocate time for relaxation, sightseeing, and social activities. Engaging in local culture and experiences not only enriches your travel experience but also provides a much-needed mental break from work. Remember, the goal of being a digital nomad is to enjoy the best of both worlds – work and travel.

Staying connected with your team and clients is vital for remote work success. Use communication tools like Slack, Zoom, and Microsoft Teams to stay in touch and participate in virtual meetings. Establish regular check-ins and update your availability to ensure smooth collaboration. Your communication helps build trust and ensures that you are aligned with your team's goals and expectations, even when you are thousands of miles away.

Adapting to different work environments is a key skill for digital nomads. You may find yourself working from a beachside café one day and a bustling city coworking space the next. Embrace this variability by being flexible and prepared. Carry essential work tools like noise-canceling headphones, portable chargers, and reliable internet access solutions. Create a checklist of your work essentials to ensure you are always prepared, regardless of your location.

Maintaining your physical and mental health is paramount while living a digital nomad lifestyle. The demands of travel and work can take a toll on your well-being if not managed properly. Incorporate regular exercise into your routine, whether it is through local gym memberships, outdoor activities, or online fitness classes. Practice mindfulness and stress-reduction techniques such as meditation or journaling to keep your mind balanced and focused. Prioritize healthy eating and sufficient sleep to stay energized and productive.

Networking and building a support system are important for thriving as a digital nomad. Connect with other remote workers through social media groups, local meetups, and coworking spaces. Sharing experiences and tips with fellow nomads can provide valuable insights and support. Networking not only helps with professional growth but also creates a sense of community and belonging, which can be comforting when you are far from home.

Finally, embrace the flexibility and opportunities that come with the digital nomad lifestyle. Use your unique position to explore diverse cultures, expand your horizons, and enhance your personal and professional development. Stay curious and open to new experiences, and continuously adapt your work practices to fit your evolving lifestyle. By maintaining a balance between work and travel, you can enjoy the freedom and adventure of being a digital nomad while continuing to achieve your professional goals.

Cultural Adaptability: Embracing and thriving in diverse cultures

Embracing and thriving in diverse cultures is a transformative experience that broadens your perspective and enriches your life. The first step in this journey is to approach new cultures with an open mind and a willingness to learn. Each culture has its unique customs, traditions, and ways of life, and being open to these differences allows you to fully appreciate and understand them. Avoid making assumptions or judgments based on your own cultural background, and instead, seek to learn and understand the reasons behind different practices and beliefs.

Immersing yourself in the local culture is essential for a deeper connection and understanding. Engage with the community by participating in local events, festivals, and everyday activities. Try local foods, learn the language, and adopt local customs. This active participation not only helps you integrate into the community but also demonstrates respect and appreciation for their way of life. The more you immerse yourself, the richer your experience will be.

Building relationships with locals is a crucial aspect of thriving in a different culture. Forming genuine connections with people from the local community can provide invaluable insights and support. Locals can offer guidance on navigating cultural nuances and help you understand the social norms and values that may not be immediately apparent. These relationships can also lead to lasting friendships and a more meaningful cultural exchange.

Being adaptable and flexible is key to thriving in a new cultural environment. Unfamiliar cultures may have different expectations, schedules, and ways of doing things. Adapting to these differences requires patience and a willingness to adjust your habits and routines. Flexibility allows you to navigate cultural challenges more smoothly and shows respect for the local way of life. Embrace the changes and view them as opportunities for personal growth and learning.

Understanding and respecting cultural differences is fundamental to successful cultural integration. Take the time to learn about the history, traditions, and values of the culture you are experiencing. This knowledge helps you navigate social interactions more effectively and avoid misunderstandings. Respecting cultural differences also involves recognizing and appreciating the diversity that exists within a culture, as not all individuals may conform to cultural stereotypes or norms.

Embracing a new culture can significantly enhance your personal development. Exposure to unusual ways of thinking and living challenges your preconceived notions and broadens your worldview. It fosters empathy, adaptability, and critical thinking, skills that are valuable in both personal and professional contexts. The experience of living and thriving in a different culture can also boost your confidence and independence, as you navigate and overcome various challenges.

Contributing to the local community is another way to thrive in a new culture. Volunteering, supporting local businesses, or participating in community projects not only benefits the community but also deepens your connection to it. Your contributions can create positive impacts and leave a legacy, making your cultural exchange experience even more rewarding. Being an active and positive member of the community helps you build a sense of belonging and purpose.

Reflecting on your cultural experiences is important for continuous learning and growth. Take time to think about what you have learned, how your perspectives have changed, and how you have adapted. Reflecting helps you internalize your experiences and apply the lessons learned to future interactions and environments. It also allows you to appreciate the journey and recognize your personal growth and achievements.

Finally, sharing your experiences with others can enrich your understanding and inspire those around you. Whether through storytelling, writing, or social media, sharing your journey of embracing and thriving in diverse cultures can foster cross-cultural understanding and appreciation. It can also serve as a source of inspiration and guidance for others who may be embarking on similar journeys. By sharing your experiences, you contribute to a more interconnected and empathetic world.

CHAPTER 12: PAYING IT FORWARD

Teaching and Mentoring: Helping others start their own journeys

Helping others start their own business is a deeply rewarding endeavor that requires a combination of guidance, support, and practical advice. The first step is to understand the individual's vision and goals for their business. Spend time discussing their ideas, motivations, and long-term objectives. This initial conversation helps clarify their vision and allows you to tailor your support to their specific needs. Understanding their aspirations ensures that your advice aligns with their unique vision, making the guidance more effective.

Providing knowledge and resources is crucial for budding entrepreneurs. Share valuable information about business planning, market research, and economic management. Offer access to resources such as business plan templates, financial forecasting tools, and market analysis reports. Providing these foundational tools equips aspiring entrepreneurs with the necessary knowledge to build a solid business plan. This practical support can significantly reduce the initial overwhelm and set them on a path to success.

Mentorship plays a vital role in helping others start their business. Offer to mentor them, providing ongoing advice and support throughout their entrepreneurial journey. Regular check-ins and feedback sessions can help them stay on track and navigate challenges effectively. As a mentor, share your own experiences and lessons learned to provide real-world insights. A strong mentor-mentee relationship can boost confidence and provide a safety net of support, making the journey less daunting.

Encouraging networking is another important aspect of supporting new entrepreneurs. Introduce them to industry contacts, potential clients, and other entrepreneurs. Networking helps them build valuable relationships and gain insights from others who have faced similar challenges. Attend networking events together or recommend relevant industry conferences and meetups. Building a strong professional network can open doors to opportunities, partnerships, and collaborations that are essential for business growth.

Helping others secure funding is often a critical part of starting a business. Provide guidance on the various funding options available, such as loans, grants, angel investors, and crowdfunding. Assist them in preparing pitches and business plans that appeal to potential investors. Share insights on how to manage finances, create budgets, and forecast financials accurately. Proper financial planning and securing adequate funding are crucial for the sustainability and growth of a new business.

Legal and regulatory guidance is also essential. Help aspiring entrepreneurs navigate the legal requirements for starting a business, such as registering their company, obtaining necessary licenses, and understanding tax obligations. Provide access to legal resources or recommend reputable legal professionals who can offer detailed advice. Ensuring compliance with legal and regulatory requirements protects the business and helps avoid potential legal issues down the line.

Encourage a mindset of resilience and adaptability. Starting a business comes with its fair share of challenges and setbacks. Share strategies for coping with failure, managing stress, and staying motivated. Emphasize the importance of learning from mistakes and being adaptable to changing circumstances. A resilient mindset enables entrepreneurs to persevere through challenging times and remain focused on their long-term goals.

Foster a culture of continuous learning and improvement. Encourage new entrepreneurs to seek feedback, attend workshops, and stay updated with industry trends. Recommend books, podcasts, and online courses that provide valuable business insights and skills development. Continuous learning helps them stay competitive and innovative, essential traits for business success. By promoting a growth mindset, you help them build a foundation for long-term success and adaptability.

Finally, celebrate their successes and milestones. Acknowledge and celebrate their achievements, no matter how small. Recognition and celebration boost morale and motivation, reinforcing their confidence and commitment. Whether it is launching their website, securing their first client, or reaching a financial milestone, celebrating these victories creates a positive and encouraging environment. Your support and encouragement play a crucial role in helping them stay motivated and confident in their entrepreneurial journey.

Giving Back: Philanthropy and social responsibility

Giving back through philanthropy and embracing social responsibility are powerful ways to make a positive impact on society and build a better future. The first step in this journey is understanding the importance of giving back and the various forms it can take. Philanthropy is not just about donating money; it includes volunteering time, sharing expertise, and supporting causes that matter. Recognizing the broad spectrum of ways to contribute helps tailor your efforts to your strengths and interests, making your giving more meaningful and effective.

Identifying causes that resonate with you personally is essential for sustained and impactful philanthropy. Reflect on the issues that you are enthusiastic about, whether they are related to education, health, environmental sustainability, or social justice. Aligning your philanthropic efforts with your personal values ensures a deeper commitment and a stronger desire to be effective. This alignment also helps you stay motivated and focused on your goals, even when challenges arise.

Engaging in philanthropy through your business can amplify your impact. Corporate social responsibility (CSR) initiatives allow businesses to contribute to societal well-being while enhancing their reputation and building stronger relationships with customers and communities. Implementing CSR programs, such as sustainable practices, fair labor policies, and charitable partnerships, demonstrates a commitment to ethical and responsible business practices. These initiatives can lead to increased customer loyalty and employee satisfaction, benefiting both society and the business.

Collaborating with other organizations and individuals can enhance the effectiveness of your philanthropic efforts. Partnering with established nonprofits, community groups, and other businesses can provide access to resources, expertise, and networks that amplify your impact. Collaborative efforts often lead to more comprehensive and sustainable solutions to complex social issues. By working together, you can leverage collective strengths and achieve greater outcomes than working in isolation.

Transparency and accountability are critical components of effective philanthropy. Clearly communicate your goals, strategies, and outcomes to stakeholders, including donors, beneficiaries, and the public. Transparency builds trust and credibility, ensuring that your efforts are viewed as genuine and impactful. Regularly report on progress and challenges and be open to feedback and suggestions for improvement. Accountability ensures that resources are used efficiently and that your efforts are making a real difference.

Encouraging a culture of giving within your organization or community can multiply the impact of your philanthropic efforts. Inspire employees, colleagues, and community members to get involved by promoting volunteer opportunities, matching donations, and recognizing their contributions. Creating an environment where giving back is valued and celebrated fosters a collective sense of purpose and social responsibility. This culture of giving can lead to increased engagement and a more positive and supportive community.

Education and advocacy are powerful tools for driving social change. Use your platform to raise awareness about the causes you support and educate others about the issues at hand. Advocacy efforts can include speaking at events, writing articles, or using social media to amplify your message. By educating and inspiring others, you can mobilize additional support and drive systemic change. Advocacy can also influence policies and practices, leading to broader and more lasting impacts.

Evaluating and reflecting on the impact of your philanthropic efforts is essential for continuous improvement. Regularly assess the outcomes of your initiatives to determine what is working well and what could be improved. Use data and feedback from beneficiaries to inform your strategies and make necessary adjustments. Reflecting on your impact not only enhances the effectiveness of your efforts but also provides valuable insights and learnings for future initiatives. Continuous evaluation ensures that your philanthropy remains relevant and impactful.

Remember that giving back is a lifelong commitment. Philanthropy and social responsibility are not one-time efforts but ongoing journeys that evolve over time. Stay committed to making a difference and continue to seek new ways to contribute and improve. Celebrate your successes, learn from your challenges, and remain dedicated to creating positive change. By embracing philanthropy and social responsibility, you contribute to a better world of compassion and impact.

Legacy Building: Creating something that outlasts you

Legacy building and creating something that outlasts you is a profound and fulfilling endeavor that requires vision, dedication, and strategic planning. The first step in this journey is to define what legacy means to you personally. Consider what you want to be remembered for and how you want to impact the world. Whether it is through philanthropic efforts, a successful business, a body of creative work, or contributions to your community, having a clear understanding of your legacy goals provides a solid foundation for your efforts.

One crucial aspect of legacy building is focusing on creating value that transcends your own lifetime. This often involves identifying needs or opportunities that can benefit future generations. For instance, establishing scholarships, endowments, or foundations can provide lasting support for education and innovation. These initiatives continue to impact lives long after you are gone, ensuring that your efforts contribute to enduring positive change. By creating sustainable and impactful solutions, you ensure that your legacy remains relevant and beneficial.

Investing in people is another powerful way to build

a legacy. Mentorship and knowledge sharing help cultivate the next generation of leaders, thinkers, and innovators. By investing your time and expertise in others, you empower them to achieve their potential and continue their work. This multiplier effect means that your influence extends far beyond your direct actions, as those you have mentored go on to make their own contributions to society.

Building a strong, value-driven organization can also serve as a legacy. Whether it is a business, nonprofit, or community initiative, an organization founded on principles of integrity, sustainability, and social responsibility can have a long-term impact. Such organizations can adapt and thrive long after their founders are gone, perpetuating the values and mission that were their foundation. Establishing an unclouded vision and a culture that embodies your principles is key to ensuring that your organization endures and continues to make a difference.

Documentation and storytelling are essential for preserving your legacy. Writing memoirs, creating documentaries, or even recording interviews can capture your experiences, insights, and the lessons you have learned. These records serve as a resource for future generations, providing them with guidance and inspiration. Sharing your story not only immortalizes your contributions but also offers a tangible connection to your values and experiences, helping others understand and build upon your legacy.

Philanthropy and social initiatives are effective ways to leave a lasting impact. Consider how your resources—time, money, or expertise—can address pressing social issues or support causes you are enthusiastic about. Establishing charitable foundations or contributing to significant projects can create lasting change in areas such as education, healthcare, or environmental conservation. These efforts demonstrate a commitment to improving the world, ensuring that your influence endures through the positive changes you initiate.

Innovation and creativity can also define your legacy. Pioneering innovative ideas, technologies, or artistic expressions can leave an indelible mark on your field. By pushing boundaries and challenging the status quo, you contribute to the advancement of knowledge and culture. Encouraging and supporting innovation within your sphere of influence ensures that your legacy includes a spirit of curiosity and progress, inspiring others to continue exploring and creating.

Community involvement is a key element of a lasting legacy. Engaging with and supporting your community fosters strong relationships and a sense of belonging. Initiatives such as community centers, local projects, or civic engagement programs can create long-term benefits for the people around you. These efforts help build a resilient and connected community that thrives on mutual support and shared values, perpetuating your impact on a local level.

Finally, reflecting on and reassessing your legacy-building efforts is crucial for sustained impact. Regularly evaluate the effectiveness and relevance of your initiatives to ensure they continue to align with your goals and values. Stay adaptable and open to new opportunities for making a difference. By continuously refining your approach and remaining committed to your vision, you ensure that your legacy is not only lasting but also dynamic and evolving, capable of meeting the needs of future generations.

CHAPTER 13: TAKE THE LEAP – STEPS TO TAKE

Taking the leap into entrepreneurship can be a transformative and rewarding journey, but it requires careful planning, resilience, and a sharp vision. Here are some steps and considerations to help you start:

1. Self-Assessment

2. Idea Generation

3. Business Planning

4. Building the Foundation

5. Marketing and Sales

6. **Launching Your Business**

7. Continuous Improvement

8. Managing Challenges

Key Takeaways

Embarking on entrepreneurship is a dynamic and ongoing process. Stay committed, flexible, and persistent as you work towards building and growing your business.

Final Encouragement: Motivational words to inspire immediate action

"Success doesn't wait for the perfect moment. Start now and create your own opportunities."

"Every great achievement begins with the decision to act. Take the first step today."

"Your dreams won't chase themselves. Get up, take action, and "The journey of a thousand miles begins with a single step. Take that step today." "Action is the bridge between your goals and your success. Cross that bridge now."

The best time "Your potential is limitless. The only thing holding you back is the decision to start."

"Great ideas are worthless without action. Take your ideas off the shelf and make them happen."

"In the world of entrepreneurship, action trumps everything. Get moving and turn your vision into reality."

Additional tools and books for continued growth

Author Ray Harding - 48 Laws of Winning

People who turned hobbies into careers

Budget University
CEO Shelby Jenkins -
budgetuniversityonline.com

Conscience Led Design
CEO Bridget Pridgen -
conscienceleddesign.com

YOU BELONG

Founder/President Kevin Hopwood - wellmentally.org

www.ingramcontent.com/pod-product-compliance
Lightning Source LLC
Chambersburg PA
CBHW050257230526
45471CB00005B/1917